# All Truth
# Is
# God's Truth

by

Arthur F. Holmes

William B. Eerdmans Publishing Company

**Library of Congress Cataloging in Publication Data**
Holmes, Arthur Frank, 1924–
    All truth is God's truth.

    1. Faith and reason. 2. Truth. 3. Christianity—
Philosophy. I. Title.
BT50.H6        201'.1        77-3567
ISBN 0-8028-1701-7

*To my students, past and present,*
*who have helped me see more clearly*
*what it means that*
*all truth is God's truth.*

# Contents

# Preface

A few years ago I reminded summer students at Regent College in Vancouver that the proposition "all truth is God's truth" underlies the Christian's educational pursuits. The idea struck a resonant chord, and I am grateful to a fellow-teacher of that summer, Canon Michael Green, for proposing this little book on the subject.

It is addressed not only to students but to thinking people everywhere who wrestle with the relation of Christianity to human learning. It is not primarily a philosophical essay, although it inevitably gets into epistemology. It is primarily an essay on faith and reason, and a summons to rest our intellectual hopes on the God who revealed himself in Jesus Christ.

Chapters one through four deal with the idea of truth; chapters five through seven with human reason as our means of getting at truth. Chapters four, six, and seven are the most detailed, and some readers may choose to skip them. They are, however, essential to the overall exposition, and I can only point out that one cannot handle the philosophical problems that underlie every subject without doing philosophy, however simplified it may be for the layman's consumption. The method I have employed is expository: I have tried to set forth a coherent view rather than trying to prove each point and defend it against all comers. My concern is that we understand how all the truth and knowledge we can ever gain come from God and bear witness to him.

I am indebted to colleagues who read and criticized the manuscript and offered helpful suggestions: Mark Coppenger, Stephen Evans, and Stanley Obitts.

# All Truth
# Is
# God's Truth

# ONE

# The Lost World-View

In Massachusetts one summer my wife and I spent a day exploring Boston's historic "Freedom Trail." Wandering from one site to another, we missed the right road and found ourselves in the Italian section amidst a lively fiesta. It was a modern version of an old-world celebration in which the community prayed together for the safe return of its fishermen. But no evidence remained of such a religious view of life.

As a teenager I visited the indoor market of the English city of Gloucester, where for centuries the farmers have brought their produce to sell. Over its ancient gate a Biblical text is inscribed: "The earth is the Lord's, and the fulness thereof." The religious note rings strangely in modern ears.

Anyone who travels the European countryside can spot a distant town by the church spires that point above fields and trees and houses toward the heavens. Around the church clusters the whole life of the town: its guild houses and its street market, its proud dwellings and its humble cottages. The finest of statuary adorns the church façade and its rose windows remind us of a bygone age when men dedicated their work and their creative art to God.

The American visitor to Oxford or Cambridge is often so accustomed to thinking of higher education in purely secular terms that he may be surprised at such college names as Corpus Christi, Emmanuel, or Trinity. Forgetting the history of our culture, he is not aware that education was once a prime concern of the church both in Europe and in America. One famous American university founded as late as the mid-nineteenth century bears in its motto the words QUAECUMQUE SUNT VERA ("whatsoever things are true") as a reminder, needed now more than originally, that all truth in every discipline is worthy of attention, for it all comes ultimately from God.

Modern man has lost the religious view of life which these observations recall. When Hellenistic culture disintegrated following the fall of the Roman Empire, a Judaeo-Christian world-view and attempts at a Christian culture gradually took its place. Politics and morality were brought together in the belief that natural law reveals the eternal law of God for his creation, a law which men and governments must obey. Art was infused with religious motivation and motifs. In the new universities theology crowned the sciences and gave a Christian focus to the understanding of man and his world. This in turn contributed, for all the troubles that ensued, to a new openness by Renaissance scientists to what they observed of the processes actually at work in God's creation. Politics, work, art, learning, science—all such human activities found a new mandate and a new basis in a Christian view of life.

Today all this sounds peculiarly anachronistic. We think instead of art and politics apart from morality, or of science in conflict with religion, for the Christian world-view has been lost and our approach to life has become fragmented. Art experiments not only with form and material but also with human morals and emotions. Jurisprudence has abandoned "the laws of nature and nature's God" (to invoke Thomas Jefferson's phrase) for pragmatic concerns unrelated to unchanging truths about man and society. Legislation reflects current sentiment rather than basic morality. Meantime technology burgeons under the incessant demands of economic growth and military power, and an ecological crisis threatens our way of life.

All this occurs at a time when overpopulation and urbanization further fragment our existence so that we desperately need, as perhaps never before, some way of seeing things as a whole. A man works in a city far from his suburban family, and his two worlds never meet. He has neither energy nor interest left over for church or cultural or civic activities, which accordingly become peripheral and leave life incomplete. He has little time for his children, and his marriage predictably falters. His many responsibilities pull him in a maze of conflicting directions without any unifying values or purpose to help him select priorities, guide each part, and unify the whole. Emotionally, and perhaps physically, he falls apart. Little wonder that the radicals of the 1960's rebelled against the rat race, and others in the counter-culture tried to cop out. "Stop the world: I want to get off" is no longer an idle joke.

Such loss of meaning is a commonplace both in contemporary literature and in existentialist philosophy. The novels and plays of Jean-Paul Sartre portray man's futile attempt to create meaning for himself. In his play *No Exit* two women and a man are confined to a room devoid of windows on the larger world and from which they cannot escape. For all their efforts to create a life of sorts together, they succeed only in alienating themselves from each other: it is a hell, and "hell is other people"; each of us ultimately stands alone without understanding or love or anything to make life meaningful and whole.

In his philosophical writings Sartre develops the theme more plainly. What a man aims to become and the meaning he seeks "for himself" are constantly negated by the alien world in which he lives, a world of people and things that he cannot effectively master because it already is "in itself" what it is.[1] Neither talk nor action nor sexual and sadistic domination of others nor anything else can ultimately succeed, and the death that finally claims a man mocks his every hope. Yet in all good faith he cannot live without doing something to give life focus. He is like a man adrift in a boat without rudder or compass, on an ocean that has no bounds. It makes no eventual difference what he does or which way he rows. But row he must, if life is to be kept together for the unpredictably little while that it lasts.

Religion offers Sartre no hope. In fact, underlying his pessimism is an outright denial of the existence of God. Did God exist, there would be limits and laws and cosmic guarantees of ultimate meaning and hope. But Sartre denies all this. He admits no moral law, no eternal purpose, no rational universe, no unchanging human self. All eternal truth is gone. The future lies wide open to any possibility of any sort. He quotes Dostoyevsky: "If God is dead then anything is possible." And the freedom this gives man is dreadful.

Sartre is more clear-sighted about the role of theistic belief than

---

1. "For himself" (le pour-soi) and "in itself" (l'en-soi) become technical terms in his major philosophical work, *Being and Nothingness,* where they stand for two kinds of existence and become the poles of a dialectical clash of opposites from which no synthesis emerges.

many of his more religious contemporaries. Either God exists and thereby guarantees life's meaning and wholeness, or else God does not exist, religion is irrelevant, and life falls apart. Too often these alternatives get mixed up: people who believe God exists either think of religion as peripheral to the life that absorbs them or else look on "secular" things as peripheral to their religion. Even the modern religious man has largely lost the religious unity of life.

## 1. The loss of truth

Our loss of the Judaeo-Christian world-view may of course be traced to multiple causes, both historical and philosophical. In this book I want to single out one cause, a largely philosophical one, and to propose some correctives which can help us recover a unifying Biblical view.

The problem I have in mind is that men and women no longer believe in truth. It is not simply that they no longer believe Christianity to be true—that is obvious—but rather that an adequate conception of truth itself is largely lost. The problem is threefold.

First, there is a *loss of focus on truth*. People are not basically concerned about truth. If their lives have any focus at all, it tends to be hedonistic (they are more concerned with their own enjoyment) or economic (making money is the most important thing). The university student is more likely to find his kicks in drugs or sex than in an all-absorbing quest for truth. Or he may regard the problem of truth as a technical philosophical inquiry unrelated to his own academic work. A pervasive pragmatism and the pressure of a hundred demands divert his time and energies elsewhere. For others, the call is more for instant relevance today than for the unchanging truth that shapes ten thousand tomorrows.

The only truth people today are likely to be concerned about is ethical: truth in lending or honesty in politics. A true world-view and the relation to God of human learning in the arts and sciences—these are usually far from the contemporary mind, or else they are regarded as optional matters of opinion rather than essential matters of pressing urgency for all education and culture.

Second, there is a *loss of the universality of truth*. Relativism is popular today. People readily adopt the view that truth is not normative for everyone but changes from time to time or place to place, even from one person to another. We meet it in the acceptance of "meaningful" religious experiences without critical examination of whether or not the underlying religious teachings are true. We find it in the theological relativism of Tillich or Bultmann, and in the situation ethics of Joseph Fletcher. Many social scientists assume that our ideas and values are relative to the cultural, psychological, or historical situations in which they arise and can make no claim to being universally true. The distinction between true and false has accordingly grown blurred: the use of these terms is largely confined to statements of fact that allow empirical confirmation, so that to speak of religious truth and moral truth and a true world-view invites criticism. Religion and morality and world-views are supposed to be somehow "beyond truth and error."

The loss may be traced in large measure to nineteenth and twentieth century reactions against the excesses of the Enlightenment in detaching the rational quest for truth from personal faith and concern. Previously the two were closely associated. Augustine's dictum "understanding is faith's reward" recognized that the quest for universal truth is essential to both faith and reason. Thomists insist that the truth reason discovers is supplemented by revealed truth to which faith assents. But Enlightenment thinkers exalted detached inquiry and scientific objectivity as the norm for human knowledge of all sorts. They wrote about politics and morality and religion as if they were purely and objectively rational undertakings, devoid of "enthusiasm" and independent of personal faith. Thomas Paine's *Age of Reason,* Immanuel Kant's *Religion Within the Limits of Reason Alone,* and Alexander Pope's *Essay on Man* are classic examples. This ideal even penetrated music, where Mozart stressed a perfection of form and technique whose objective rational order restrains any unbridled outburst of emotion.

Undoubtedly, there is need for objectivity in our thinking, and personal concerns can distort our understanding and thereby engender relativism. But we must still keep personal concern related to the quest for truth. Enlightenment thinkers obscured this relationship because they overlooked an important distinction between two meanings of "objective" and "subjective." The first meaning may be illustrated by Descartes' view (although he did not use the terms this way) that ideas occurring within the mind ("subjective") represent things outside the mind ("objective"). A belief is thus said to be "purely subjective" when it does not represent any objective reality at all; and if it is "objective" it is not relative at all but universally the same for every human subject. Since "objective" here refers to objective realities, we shall call it "metaphysical objectivity."

The second meaning is illustrated by Kierkegaard's discussion of the act of believing and the way in which we approach the truth. We can approach it in a detached and impersonal way ("objectively") or else passionately, in a personally concerned way ("subjectively"). Religious faith is clearly subjective, in this sense, as is the virtue of love practiced by Christ and taught in the New Testament. Since "objective" and "subjective" here refer to the act and attitude of knowing, we shall speak of "epistemological objectivity" and "epistemological subjectivity."

The important point which I want to stress, and which the Enlightenment missed, is that metaphysical objectivity is perfectly compatible with epistemological subjectivity. I can passionately believe in a certain objective reality without at all violating either my intellectual integrity or the universality of truth. I can believe in God, I can love my neighbor as myself, and I can accept a Christian world-view with all the subjective intensity of my being without compromising in the least the universal truth of theism, of Christian ethics, and of a Christian world-view. I believe all truth is God's truth, passionately so, but that does not make it any less objectively real.

The Enlightenment failed to appreciate this distinction. It confined itself to objectivity, both metaphysical and epistemological. By insisting that reason requires epistemological objectivity, it failed to relate faith (i.e., epistemological subjectivity) effectively to reason's quest for universal truth (i.e., metaphysical objectivity). By admitting as true only impersonal statements of what is either logically necessary or a demonstrable fact, it allowed David Hume and other writers with sceptical inclination to relegate things of personal concern, like morality and religion and world-views, to the domain of feeling rather than reason, and so contributed to the tendency that places them today "beyond truth and error."

Nineteenth century romanticism reacted against the epistemological objectivity of this rationalism by enthroning the emotive dimensions of art, morality, and religion, and such existentialists as Nietzsche and Sartre turned from the rule of reason to the passionate rule of the will. The late twentieth century, therefore, finds a great gulf fixed between the demand for logical proof or objectively verifiable statements of fact, on the one hand, and the romanticist and existentialist reactions, on the other. In the one, objective reason rules and universal truth is affirmed, while in the other the personal has primacy and the universality of truth seems lost. What remains lacking is a view of truth that combines the two, one which combines universal truth (metaphysical objectivity) with free personal commitment (epistemological subjectivity). My contention in this book is that a Christian view of truth can meet this need without lapsing into Enlightenment rationalism on the one hand, or into either existentialism or romanticism on the other hand. Personal faith, I insist, is compatible with the careful and critical examination of evidence.

The third problem we face is a *loss of the unity of truth*. In a *uni*verse subject to the rule of one creator-God, as in any other unified world-view, truth is seen as an interrelated and coherent whole. Sometimes we interrelate things mistakenly, and only Christianity sees everything in relation to the creator-God revealed to us in Jesus Christ. But whenever the focus on truth is lost, our loss includes the unity of truth; and when the universality of truth is lost, it includes the universal truth of any one unifying world-view. What then happens to truth in relation to art and morals, to truth in politics and business? We are left with fragmented items devoid of any ultimate coherence.

One contributing factor to this incoherence is the tendency to ascribe truth just to particular statements of fact and to limit the quest for truth to empirical methods patterned on those of the natural sciences. We shall therefore have to examine the claims of empiricism, as well as of alternative methods of knowing, and to ask how far they lead to the unity and universality of truth.

Our agenda will therefore expose us to questions about truth and error, about faith and reason, about logic and various theories of knowledge, and it will expose us to ways in which the truth of a world-view touches various areas of life and learning. In it all, our concern will be to develop a Christian view of truth that is consonant with Biblical theology and that meets the needs we have described. Such a view of truth is not new. It is rooted in Scripture and it has guided Christian thought, although it contrasts strongly with the loss of truth in our day.

## 2. All truth is God's truth

The early church claimed that all truth is God's truth wherever it be found. The *focus* here is on truth. But the ultimate *locus* of truth is God. If he is the eternal and all-wise creator of all things, as Christians affirm, then his creative wisdom is the source and norm of all truth about everything. And if God and his wisdom are unchangingly the same, then truth is likewise unchanging and thus *universal*. If all truth is his, and he understands fully its interrelatedness, then truth is *unified* in his perfect understanding. The threefold loss of truth which we have noted is thereby overcome in God.

This claim must be plainly understood. It is a statement primarily about God's understanding, not man's. For man, it is a confession of faith and an essential part of the Christian *credo*. When we recite the Apostles' Creed ("I believe in God the Father Almighty, maker of heaven and earth...."), we tacitly affirm that the creator of all knows all about his creation so that all truth about everything is his, and he knows it all as a coherent whole. We do not affirm that everything men take to be true is God's truth.

To say that all truth is God's truth, moreover, does not mean that all truth is either contained in the Bible or deducible from what we find there. Historic Christianity has believed in the truthfulness of Scripture, yet not as an *exhaustive* revelation of everything men can know or want to know as true, but rather as a *sufficient* rule for faith and conduct. Human knowledge in mathematics and science has arisen from other sources than Biblical teachings. Historical and philosophical knowledge overlap here and there with Biblical knowledge: but there is no Biblical history of modern Europe nor any Biblical theory of sense perception, to cite two obvious examples. At a more trivial level, what about the knowledge that I am writing these words with a black pen at 12:20 p.m. on October 23? The statement is true, but it is neither found in the Bible nor deducible therefrom. Yet, we say, "God knows it's true." That is no idle piece of rhetoric, for all truth is ultimately known to God and so may be called "God's truth" whether it be found in the Bible or elsewhere.

Nor does it mean that the Christian or anybody else can readily grasp what is unchangingly true, or tie everything together, understand fully all the interrelationships, and resolve every apparent difficulty. No man is omniscient. The unity and universality of truth pose an ideal for human knowledge, but they do not necessarily describe the present state of affairs that actually prevails in our understanding. We are speaking of a universality and unity which we strive to approximate in our thinking, not describing the perfection of present knowledge. It remains the case that "we know in part" and "see through a glass darkly."

But at the same time, this *credo* about truth extends hope to man that truth is knowable and life ultimately makes sense. It means that men created as intelligent beings in God's image can hope to understand in measure a world intelligently made by the most intelligent being of all. It means that although we know in part and see it all dimly, yet what we see and know will ideally fit together into the intelligible whole God himself knows it to be. And this glimpse of the unity and universality of truth gradually generates in more detail a unified world-view.

That all truth is God's truth is implicit in the Old Testament understanding that all of life and history is known to and governed by a good, wise, and powerful creator. The first twelve chapters of the book of Genesis recount the development of human culture from the resources of creation, and tell of God's concern about man's perverted use of things. Mosaic legislation concerned matters of bodily health as well as morality, the artistry of the tabernacle as well as its religious functions, a civil justice that protects the underprivileged and falsely accused, and an economic structure that would not perpetuate abject poverty. The psalmist saw all of nature and history as God's doing. Job struggled, as the blows fell, to understand his sufferings; he forsook every other point of reference in his thinking except the sovereign providence of God. The writer of Ecclesiastes wrestled with the value of wealth, family, learning, and leisure, and found such things vacuous apart from the fact that they are God's good gifts to men. The prophets brought the life of the nation under the judgment of God's law—its political ups and downs, its social and economic injustices, and its religious practices. In all of this, the outline of a theistic world-view becomes apparent. The truth about every area is interrelated as a coherent whole in God's wisdom, so that for man "the fear of the Lord is the beginning of wisdom." That is to say, the believer has a starting point which gives perspective on life both in its parts and as a whole.

A similar picture emerges in the New Testament. Jesus' teaching in the Gospels touches various aspects of personal and social life, and sees all history fulfilling the ultimate purposes of the one God. Subsequently, when Stephen preached to the Jewish council (Acts 7), he spoke of God's covenant with their fathers, not as a peripheral bonus added to life but as the central thread which gave significance to their nation's history and their present life. He presented Jesus not just as a promised national messiah, but as the Lord of everything. The letter to the Hebrews, concentrating as it does upon Christ's fulfillment of Old Testament religious symbolism, introduces Jesus as active in creation and as lord of creation (Heb. 1). His grace restores man to his proper place in the created order (Heb. 2). Faith is not an unrelated addendum to life: it touches all kinds of things (Heb. 11), restores hope and meaning amidst suffering (Heb. 12), generates compassion for the needy (13:1-3), respect for marriage and a right assessment of material things (13:4-5). The New Testament thus poses an overall world-view that brings everything into focus around the lordship of Christ, the divine creator.

The most explicit Biblical statement on the subject is Paul's letter to the Colossian church in response to a conflicting religious world-view. While the exact identity of that Colossian heresy is the subject of considerable debate, it was seemingly a Jewish version of the Gnostic movements current in early Christian centuries. Its central teachings, the "mystery" revealed to its initiates, were threefold: (1) a hierarchy of intermediary beings ("principalities and powers") stands between God and man, emanating from the divine being and ordering the physical creation; (2) man's bodily existence is in itself so disarranged and so removed from the perfection of God that it detracts from knowing God and handicaps the practice of moral virtue; (3) man's hope of deliverance from evil lies in an ascetic denial of the body and a mystic ascent via the intermediary beings to reunion with God (Col. 2:18-23).

All three of these teachings were evidently in Paul's mind when he wrote to Colosse. He responds to the first teaching by rejecting the doctrine of intermediary emanations. Jesus Christ is no intermediary being but the creator-God himself who made all things in heaven and on earth, including whatever principalities and powers exist. All things exist by him and for him (1:15–17). Contrary to the second teaching, the source of evil is not in the material body as such, but in the wilful alienation of the human mind from God (1:21; cp. I Tim. 4:1–5). Accordingly Paul rejects the third teaching, asceticism and mysticism. He speaks instead of reconciliation to God by the *bodily* incarnation and death of Jesus Christ—an impossibility if the body is itself evil (1:18–22). The Christian should therefore approach the present life constructively, seeking peace and reconciliation with others rather than pursuing selfish interests or allowing alienation to persist (3:5–16). He should work wholeheartedly at his family relationships and economic tasks, for these too are a part of God's mandate to his creatures (3:17–4:1).

This outline of Paul's response summarizes the rudiments of a world-view that appears less explicitly throughout Scripture. The apostle warned his readers about philosophy in the Gnostic tradition, and speaks instead of one rooted in our knowledge of Jesus Christ (the language of 2:8 plainly indicates a certain kind of philosophy, not philosophy in general). He implies the possibility of an all-embracing Christian philosophy of life.

One expression he uses is often misconstrued. He says that in Christ "are hid all the treasures of wisdom and knowledge" (2:3). In the first place the term "hid" does not imply that the truth is inaccessible or unintelligible to men. Rather it carries the metaphor of mystery introduced earlier in the same sentence, the Christian "mystery" that has now been made known (1:26–27) and is intelligible to men (2:2). This Christian "mystery" stands in contrast to the Gnostic "mystery," and is revealed in that Jesus Christ is the divine creator and lord of all.

In the second place, the expression does not imply that he who knows Christ has a royal road to learning everything else worth knowing. A person who adopts such an interpretation still listens to the latest news or sports results, and he still needs to know about the arts and sciences. The point is not to exclude certain kinds of knowledge but to include it all. Everything is known to the divine creator, and in his perfect understanding all wisdom and knowledge form an interrelated whole. Truth is one.

But there is still more to it than this. Paul's main point in

Colossians is not that Christ is omniscient, but that the truth about Christ is the focal center to which all other truth about everything in creation is ultimately connected. Whatever we understand about nature is ultimately about his creative wisdom and power; whatever we do in human art and science ultimately comes from the creative and rational potential that God invested in men by making us in his own image. To understand this centrality of Jesus Christ in all knowledge gives perspective to moral and social issues, to interpersonal relations, marriage, and work, in fact to everything in all the arts and sciences of men. With a unified view like this, we can think whole.

The same theme appears, though less plainly to the modern mind, in the Johannine writings of the New Testament. The prologue to the Fourth Gospel speaks of Jesus Christ as the *Logos,* the Word. Once again the term evokes comparisons with other philosophical ideas, for it was used by a variety of ancient writers: yet by his selection of this term, John plainly wishes to speak of what they sought to understand. Heraclitus of Ephesus (d. 475 B.C.) used *Logos* of a rational element in nature, so that what would otherwise be a confusing and chaotic flux becomes an intelligible and ordered process. The *Logos,* moreover, is associated with human intelligence and its power to think soundly and give to life the guidance of reason. Anaxagoras (d. *circa* 428 B.C.) employed the synonym *Nous,* or Mind, in related ways. It too is a rational principle at work in nature, holding things together which otherwise would fall apart, and making them intelligible to man. The term *Logos* appears similarly in the Stoics for an active and rational force that controls the material elements and gives to nature its ordered unity. The *Logos* is a life-giving principle diffused throughout nature, and a seminal deposit of it comprises each man's soul. The Alexandrian Jew, Philo (d. 50 A.D.), viewed the *Logos* as the sum of all the intermediary beings emanating from God, as the shaper of the universe, the divine reason diffused among men.

Each of these *Logos* concepts becomes the focus of a germinal world-view, but the Biblical usage goes further. It presents the *Logos* as coeternal and coequal with God, and as the personal creator who transcends the world he makes from nothing. "In the beginning was the Word" (John 1:1) echoes the opening words of Genesis: "In the beginning God created . . . and God said. . . ." In Hebrew thought a word is not a detached comment, but a creative act, a decree that effects what it declares (cp. Ps. 33:8–9; Isa. 55:10–11). John's *Logos* also recalls the personified wisdom who governs the nations, rewards the just, and existed from the beginning of creation (Prov. 8:14–31). He who finds such wisdom finds life (Prov. 8:35). John therefore declares that the *Logos* is personal, and one with God; he is creator of all, and he gives life and light to men. By incarnating himself, he revealed both grace and truth (John 1:1–14). John's *Logos,* and the Biblical world-view of which John's *Logos* is the focus, thereby stand in marked contrast to their extra-Biblical parallels.

John elaborates his claim in the remainder of his Gospel, introducing Christ as the one who makes men whole and restores meaning to broken and twisted lives. Similarly he begins his first epistle, in words that echo the "in the beginning" of Genesis and of his Gospel, by declaring the bodily reality of the *Logos* made flesh, in the face of Gnostic and other views which depreciated the body. The incarnation of the *Logos* reaffirms the worth and meaningfulness of our bodily life. The epistle accordingly calls those who believe this to a life of love expressed in proper bodily behavior and in concern for others' well-being. It is little wonder that in all three of his epistles, John denounces those who reject the reality of Christ's bodily incarnation, for thereby they implicitly reject the entire Christian view of creation and redemption, and so of life itself. The Apocalypse too refers to Christ coming to rule the nations of earth as "the Word of God" (Rev. 19:13).

The *Logos* doctrine is further developed by the early church fathers. Tatian, for example, points out that just as he who speaks does not thereby separate himself from his speech (*logos*) but rather tries to bring order to the disarranged minds of his hearers, so the divine *Logos* is not separated from the Godhead, but remains the fully divine creator.[2] The same emphasis persisted in Augustine and the medievals, so that as late as Thomas Aquinas (d. 1274) Christ is seen as the divine *Logos* who orders all things by his wisdom, and in whose rational image men are made. We shall return to this conception in a later chapter.

The church fathers find in the *Logos* their explanation not only of the order of creation in general, but also of the rationality of

---

2. Tatian's *Address to the Greeks,* v.

man and his potential for grasping truth. The *Logos* is revealed both in the Incarnation and in the written words of Scripture and, if less specifically, in the intelligible order of his creation. Hence non-Christians as well as Christians perceive the truth, if fragmentarily. All truth, no matter where it be found or by whom it be discovered, is still God's truth.

Clement of Alexandria declares:

> Truth is one . . . all, in my opinion, are illuminated by the dawn of light. . . . The barbarian and Hellenic philosophy has torn off a fragment of eternal truth not from the mythology of Dionysius but from the theology of the ever-living Word.

> [Even] if the Hellenic philosophy comprehends not the whole extent of the truth, and besides is destitute of strength to perform the commandments of the Lord, yet it prepares the way for the truly royal teaching. . . .[3]

Justin Martyr wishfully thinks that Plato may have borrowed some of his insights from a reading of Moses, but he explicitly denies that men can learn true religion and the message of salvation outside of the inspired Biblical witness. He sees the divine *Logos* as somehow the source of whatever truth Plato or Socrates or Heraclitus or the Stoics may have apprehended.

> For each man spoke well in proportion to the share he had of the spermatic word, seeing what was related to it. . . . Whatever things are rightly said among all men are the property of us Christians. For next to God, we worship and love the Word.[4]

The Scriptures and the church fathers clearly placed the focus on truth, they perceived its universality, and they recognized the ultimate unity of all truth in God. They believed, passionately so, that all truth is God's truth no matter where it be found. Yet today the Christian faith is too often seen as a private affair of the heart without reference to the larger scope of human knowledge and cultural affairs. Such a faith is too small to match the understanding which the early church had of the message of Scripture. God is creator and lord of all; Jesus Christ reaffirms this by becoming incarnate to redeem human life. For the Christian, then, all of life

---

3. *Stromata,* I.xiii, xvi.
4. *Second Apology,* xiii.

matters and all of thought. All our learning must somehow fit together. Of course, "now we know in part" and we see these things "through a glass darkly." But the Christian gospel of hope pertains among other things to our knowing and understanding the truth.

# TWO

# Sacred and Secular

In the first chapter we saw some of the reasons for today's loss of the unity and universality of truth and contrasted with that the lost claim that all truth is God's. We want now to look at objections which Christians sometimes raise to the unity of truth and to the kind of involvement which that implies for us, particularly at attempts to dichotomize "secular" and "sacred" concerns.

A number of years ago, while walking along the street with a book in my hand, I met a retired minister whom I had seen occasionally in church. We stopped to pass the time of day, and he inquired what I was carrying. I showed it to him: something about Einstein and the history of science. He nodded with muted interest and said, "Ah, yes, the wisdom of this world."

We could trade stories for a long time about the suspicion with which some Christian people regard human learning. They compartmentalize "sacred" literature or "spiritual" wisdom from "secular" learning. They raise their eyebrows with incomprehension and uneasiness at the suggestion that all truth is God's truth wherever it be found. They divorce the "spiritual" life from "secular" activities generally. Thereby they betray their lack of any unifying world-view, and tacitly deny the unity of truth.

To a considerable extent this widespread malady is psychosomatic, for it is caused by a fear of the unknown. We feel so threatened by the unfamiliar, living as we do in the shadow of past conflicts between religion and science, that we try to insulate ourselves and what we hold most dear from whatever in life or learning seems ominous. Yet this is symptomatic not only of fear, but also of a tragic misunderstanding of the nature of truth and of the Christian faith itself.

A preliminary look at the terminology will help us get the problem into focus.

"Sacred" is often used in this context for distinctively religious matters. Actually the term refers to what is holy in the sense that it is or should be dedicated to God, and in that sense everything in creation should be treated as holy, and nothing may be withheld from him. All of life's activities, its work and its play, science and art, are therefore sacred and it is a mistake to compartmentalize the sacred as we often do.

"Religious" is often used of activities such as worship and prayer and church-related work, and Roman Catholics apply it to those who have taken vows and joined a religious order. But the word probably derives, like our word "rely," from the Latin *religare,* which means "to tie back"; it speaks of conscientiousness about everything in life, and of regard for God in everything we do. Compartmentalization is therefore precluded.

"Spiritual" adds an emphasis on inner aspects of the religious life, such as personal faith and private devotion. Yet in the New Testament, the "spiritual man" is one whose whole life and thought are open to the transforming grace of God's Spirit. No one area is marked off as spiritual, for whatever we do, in word or deed, we are to do from the heart and for the Lord.

"Secular" is used by way of contrast to "spiritual" or "sacred" or "religious," to refer to the temporal affairs of this world; Roman Catholics use it of persons who are not members of religious orders. Of course, the Reformation belief in the priesthood of all believers places the same demands for faith and devotion on all Christians regardless of their work. Yet the double standard which Protestants deny in regard to "orders" they frequently seem to affirm by separating the sacred from the secular. Religion is not a matter of church activities or of the inner dimension only, an enriching addendum without which things might conceivably go along just as intelligibly as with it, nor is the secular a second-rate citizen in the kingdom of God.

At the verbal level, then, it is difficult to sustain the popular dichotomy. The terminological difficulties suggest that no adequate reason may exist for isolating the sacred or for denigrating the secular.

## 1. Reasons for divorce

With this preamble in mind, we begin to wonder how such dichotomies arise and what people have to fear from the "secular." They arise, I think, from a fear of compromising the faith

by identifying it with the current and the cultural. Such "worldliness" silences the word of God that transcends current beliefs
and practices and that brings all of life and culture under the
judgment and the grace of God.

Reactions against a compromising identification appear in relation to political and social involvement as well as theological
beliefs. Tertullian, for instance, spoke out in the early church
against Christian participation in governmental and military affairs and against many of the social practices of the day, and
some have argued that the church forfeited its early purity when it
joined forces with the Roman Empire. When the Middle Ages
wedded church and state and thereby identified the church with
the social and political *status quo,* reforming and separatist
movements arose: Franciscan, Waldensian, and others. In post-
Reformation times, the Anabaptists refused to participate in many
governmental tasks because of the social and moral compromises
they saw it would involve. In nineteenth century Denmark, Søren
Kierkegaard protested vigorously against a state church wherein
one became a Christian willy-nilly by being born a Dane. And in
the past few years, some of the "Jesus people" have repudiated
the church's identification with what they see as an effete
middle-class "establishment" and have developed a "counter-
culture" life-style instead.

All these reactions are essentially counter-cultural, and each in
its time contributed needed perspective to the life of the church.
To identify the church with any historical *status quo* is a tragic
betrayal of the church's calling. To accept uncritically the structures of the present betrays a weakened doctrine of sin and loses
that holy discontent which is always hungry for righteousness.

To identify Christianity with a historical culture loses sight of
transcendent moral law. That the moral practices and social institutions of the day have been too easily hallowed by the church
is evident in regard to war, slavery, work, sex, marriage, the
status of women, and, especially in America, a capitalist economy and democratic institutions. Rather than uncritically assuming that current principles and practices are fully Christian because they were influenced along the way by Christian ideas and
because they seem better than some other alternatives, we should
rather keep every moral practice and social institution under the
constant judgment of God's law and constantly seek better ways
of implementing that law in everyday life.

In theological matters also, the history of heresy is largely the history of identification of the faith with current religious and philosophical ideas. The Christological heresies of the first four or five centuries of church history, for example, resulted from the adoption of Gnostic and Platonic ideas into Christian theology. Deism grew out of Enlightenment ideas. The liberal theology of the nineteenth century stemmed from a too-easy identification of Christianity with idealist and romanticist philosophy.[1] Theological examples could be multiplied many times over, and one could add tensions between theology and the various sciences, especially cosmology, biology, and now psychology. It is not at all surprising that some react against this series of mis-identifications by trying to insulate Christianity altogether from "secular" influence.

A total separation would be difficult to achieve. The church may not be *of* the world but it still is *in* the world, inevitably employing cultural language and thought-structures, and its members are inevitably involved to some degree in its social and economic life whether or not they involve themselves in its politics. The problem that divides Christians is rather one of policy. Should we withdraw as much as we possibly can, so as to preserve the purity of our Christian distinctives from worldliness, or should we seek to penetrate the "secular" at all levels with Christian perspectives? Can the Christian contribute anything to the secular world except an ultimate hope? Does the Great Commission exhaustively define our vocation, or has God also given us a cultural mandate?

## 2. Is the secular worldly?

Some religious groups, we have indicated, regarded secular culture as "worldly" and equated secular learning with "the wisdom of the world." This was true of certain monastic movements in their studied withdrawal from society, although some other monasteries became centers of learning and repositories of ancient manuscripts. Some Anabaptist and holiness groups have in

---

1. This kind of process is described by Colin Brown in *Philosophy and the Christian Faith* (Tyndale Press, 1969). Alternative attitudes of Christians to culture are discussed by Richard Niebuhr in *Christ and Culture* (Harper Torchbooks, 1951).

the past made a virtue of non-involvement in politics and governmental affairs and have been suspicious of education.

Christians are not the only ones to practice cultural withdrawal. The Cynics of ancient Greece, disillusioned with political and domestic institutions, tried to return to nature by means of a simple life free from dependence on the accoutrements and structures that society thought needful. More recently the Hippies and other counter-culture movements adopted a similar attitude, and segments of the Jesus movement share both their cynicism of the establishment and their simplified values and life-styles.

Yet we have seen in recent years that a counter-culture is itself a culture, creating its own moral and social expectations and evolving its own economic and political structures. Cultural involvement cannot be avoided no matter how well we may avoid enslavement to one culture or another. Consider the Amish groups of Pennsylvania and Indiana that refuse to conform to twentieth century expectations. They drive horses rather than cars, use oil lamps rather than electricity, shun modern dress and all but elementary education; yet they have a highly developed authority structure of their own. They employ cultural accoutrements from the past, practice arts and crafts, and make full use of what learning they have. Their withdrawal is pragmatic: it preserves group identity and guards against the self-indulgence of needless luxury and learning, but it does not and cannot exclude the "secular" tasks which economic and domestic and social needs demand of us all. Man is a cultural being: his culture is the way he goes about meeting his needs and enriching his life. He may reject current practices and institutions, but that is not to reject culture as such. He cannot reject cultural tasks without rejecting himself.

The question, rather, is whether the arts and sciences are of value for any but pragmatic purposes—whether it is a legitimate endeavor or merely human pride to beautify life with art and ennoble it with learning. The answer depends on whether we value nature and man in themselves, whether we value the creative potential of man more than we fear his tendency to pride, or whether sin destroys the possibility of making culture as well as nature bear witness to the truth and glorify God.

I have no trouble answering this question. Nature and man bear the imprint of their creator. God made nature intelligible and beautiful to behold, and he endowed man with the capacity for creating beauty and acquiring knowledge himself. In these regards, at least, man is uniquely in the image of his creator, as his artistic and intellectual activities bear witness. Understanding and creativity, as well as righteousness, are of intrinsic value because God is wise and creative as well as righteous. One can no more reject the pursuit of beauty or understanding on the grounds that they are self-indulgent exercises in pride, than he can reject the pursuit of righteousness on the grounds that it makes a man self-righteous. And it would be as superficial to value truth and beauty simply for their utility as it would be to seek righteousness just to impress God or to influence men. God's gracious gifts to his creatures are to be valued and developed, and we are to involve ourselves heartily in his creation.

The Biblical doctrine of creation makes this plain. "God saw all he had made and it was very good" (Gen. 1:31) repeats a value judgment made six times before in the first chapter of Scripture. The psalmist celebrates the wonders of God's creation, and Old Testament history makes it plain that God called gifted men to use their artistic ability for creating beauty and called learned men to share their wisdom with others. Moses was well schooled in the learning of the Egyptians, Daniel in Babylonian scholarship, Paul in the Rabbinical schools, and for all their disagreement with one or another cultural belief or practice, they did not withdraw from the learning and culture of their times. The Biblical writers themselves display the literary art with excellence and in a variety of genres, and they reveal an intimate knowledge of both nature and society.

Is the "secular" worldly? Not in the sense in which "the world" is deceptive and ensnares the believer in sin. Not in the sense that worldliness loves the creature more than the creator. Nor in the sense of conforming our attitudes and conduct to non-Christian standards rather than to the Word of God. The secular is part and parcel of creation: its tasks are "creational" tasks and as such they are good. Withdrawal from the secular appears to be neither possible nor necessary.

## 3. Is the secular beyond help?

The doctrine of creation must be qualified by the doctrine of sin. Is human culture then so deformed that secular tasks are hopeless? Can the Christian who engages in politics or art or science hope to help the sorry state of affairs? Has he anything to contribute at all to this world but God's message of forgiveness?

Jacques Ellul is a former French underground leader and mayor of Bordeaux, a law professor, and a prolific writer on sociological and theological topics. He rejects both the identification of Christianity with current cultural movements and the practice of withdrawing from the world and its problems. In *The Presence of the Kingdom* he maintains instead that the Christian is called to challenge the suicidal direction of the world by spiritual means. We cannot hope to change society, for there are no universal moral rules as a basis for political agreement between the Christian and a secular world. We must therefore learn to put up with the tension between sacred and secular, and develop a Christian life-style in response to the demand of God's kingdom upon us. Thereby we shall bear witness to the hope we have in God.

Since the Christian cannot expect to change society for the better, Ellul refuses to sanctify secular methods or theories of politics or law or violence by making up a Christian political theory or a Christian philosophy of law or a Christian justification of violence. He may have to use political or violent means as he does legal means, because he lives in this world; but they are forced on him by the necessities of history, not chosen because they are either right or Christian.

The idea of a Christian culture or a normative Christian social ethic or a Christian political theory (as distinct from a Christian critique of society) is alien to Ellul. A unified and developed world-view that articulates such ideas is therefore impossible because of human sin. From this point of view, the unity of truth is at best an impractical dream of man's unfallen past and at worst a delusion. Ellul does not spell out a concept of truth. His sociology is rigorously empirical as if truth is some sort of objectively verifiable correspondence to fact; however, his theological writings, for all their Biblical quotations, seem to present no explicit conception of truth. Empirical facts are not treated as facts of God's creation that bear witness to him, but as facts of man's making in the process of history. Ellul's doctrine of sin thus obscures both the doctrine of creation and the Biblical conception of unchanging, universal, and unified truth rooted in the God in whom we hope.

Ellul is, of course, right that the identification of Christianity with an existing social system or a current ethic ignores the reality of sin. But to regard the secular as so beyond help as to turn us to spiritual rather than creational means ignores the reality of common grace. The God who makes the sun to shine on the just and the unjust alike graciously works through the processes of nature and history to preserve in sinful men a degree of wisdom and creativity and civil righteousness, and thereby he accomplishes his present purposes in society. Whatever men do that is right and good they do by the goodness of God, for every good gift comes from above. Whatever men know they know by the grace of God, for all truth is God's truth wherever it be found.

Nor is the work of God in history limited to his common grace to all men. His saving grace to the believer touches the world too, through the influence of Christian beliefs on secular thought and Christian values on secular life. The presence of the kingdom makes itself felt not only by its eternal yet elusive hope, but also by the present reality of its creative impact in philosophy, in the arts and sciences, in political and social institutions. Secular society is firmly rooted in God's creation and in it God is still creatively at work.

I have theological difficulties, therefore, in accepting Ellul's rather pessimistic view. Neither the over-optimism of the identification theory nor the over-pessimism of Ellul's separation of sacred from secular do justice to the admixture of wheat and tares in human thought and culture. The problem of evil cannot and indeed must not be ignored—we shall return to it when we look at the problem of error—but neither may we minimize the pervasive power of God's goodness through "natural" as well as "spiritual" means. With God working creatively in men and history, the secular is not beyond help.

## 4. Is the secular important?

What is the vocation of the Christian? Does his real calling leave time or energy for secular things? This is the question of priorities. In the early church Origen excused Christians from holding political office or undertaking military service on the grounds that they had a higher calling. Christians serve the emperor by prayer and spiritual weapons rather than by political and other secular means. A doctrine of two vocations developed, the spiritual and the secular, with the spiritual eclipsing the secular in the lives of Christians.

As the church grew to include those with political and other responsibilities, the concept of the Christian's task widened, but the idea of two vocations persisted in the medieval (and still the Roman Catholic) distinction between those in religious orders and the remainder of the church. Some monastic movements accordingly turned from the world to the higher calling of cultivating an inner spiritual life through prayer and meditation. The Mennonites and Anabaptists spoke of two kingdoms, the earthly and the heavenly; they often declined to participate in the former and put all their energies into the latter. Since the earthly is of no eternal value, the Christian disciple's role in this world is one of prayerful witness to the heavenly kingdom and to the law of love which Jesus introduced.

Contemporary evangelicalism shows a similar tendency in speaking of the missionary mandate as if it were the believer's only reason for being in this world. This particular emphasis is a product of the last 150 years or so of missionary and evangelistic endeavor in which the church at large has commendably paid increased attention to the great commission, stressing both foreign missions and personal witness to Jesus Christ. The missionary mandate is, however, not the only mandate God gave men, nor is it limited to evangelism.

In the first place, the missionary mandate as recorded in Matthew's gospel contains one explicit imperative—to make disciples. The other verbs (going, baptizing, and teaching) are participles that prescribe how discipling is to be done. Discipleship is a broader and more complex task than evangelism: it means conforming the whole person and his whole life to the will of God. Social and intellectual and artistic activities are thereby included.

In the second place, the missionary mandate is not our only mandate, nor was it the first. God commissioned man at creation to invest his life and work in *creational* tasks, by superintending and making wise use of the resources of nature (Gen. 1:27–28). This creation mandate was never repealed, despite the intrusion of sin, for the eighth Psalm still holds man to it. The New Testament (Heb. 2:6–8) cites that Psalm, acknowledging the creation mandate and noting that, while sinful men fail to fulfil it, the redeeming work of Christ restores us to its tasks. Subsequently, men of faith are cited (in Hebrews 11) for their cultural and historical deeds, and Hebrews 12–13 speaks of Christian responsibility for human relations generally and especially for people in need. Even sex and marriage are regarded as sacred. Christianity does not exempt us from the creation mandate with its cultural and ''secular'' responsibilities but brings us to it with all the perspective and grace that Jesus Christ provides.

This is evident throughout Scripture. From the agrarian life of the patriarchs to the political responsibilities of judges and kings, the Old Testament is replete with accounts of ''secular'' work. The Mosaic legislation touches every area of life, and none is exempt from the prophets' scrutiny. Jesus himself did ''secular'' work until he was 30, and his silent years bear mute testimony to its sanctity. The apostle Paul's teaching touches political and economic life and all sorts of human relationships because they are inseparable from his missionary task in the church. The missionary, like the prophet, is called to proclaim the word of God and apply it to all of life by what he says. The politician and the educator, like the king, are called to infuse the law and truth of God into the daily practice of ''secular'' life and learning.

We must not mistake one part of life's responsibility for the whole. What then is the highest end of man that unifies all of life's parts? The Westminster Shorter Catechism answers the question: ''the highest end of man is to glorify God and to enjoy him for ever.'' Jesus taught that the first and great commandment is that we should love the Lord God with all our being. Glorifying God and loving him are not confined to directly religious activities, but find expression in all a man does when he does it heartily ''as unto the Lord.'' Likewise, to ''seek first the kingdom of God and his righteousness'' is to extend the lordship of Christ and the law of God into every area of life. The Christian's calling is an all-inclusive one, not one that excludes ''secular'' parts and pieces. It includes evangelism and witness, essentially so, but it also includes the family and politics, art and intellectual pursuits. Nothing is excluded and nothing is of such secondary importance that it can be omitted from Christian concern.

Of course, each individual has peculiar gifts and tasks that define his personal priorities within the whole. My own seem to identify me as a teacher and scholar. By that token it would be irresponsible of me to neglect those gifts and needlessly to expend my limited time and energy on things tangential to the main task. But those things which are tangential to my task may be central in somebody else's calling. What is given primary or secondary attention depends on a person's peculiar calling, rather than on the overall calling of Christians to glorify God in all their creaturely activities.

The idea of Christian witness, like discipleship and vocation, is too often narrowed down to what is in fact but one part of witnessing, namely a verbalized testimony to the saving work of Christ. Just as discipleship extends to every area of life and the vocation of the Christian is to glorify God in all he is and does, so Christian witness is all-inclusive. I am not speaking now of the witness of a person's conduct, although that too is included. Rather all creation bears witness to the creator's power and wisdom. The Christian likewise witnesses by the breadth and depth of his involvement in God's creation. Whatever he is and does speaks concerning truth, and all truth is God's truth wherever it be found. All creaturely activities and all human learning bear witness.

The Biblical doctrine of work has the same impact. Work is not a necessary evil, something essential to earning a living but without any other redeeming value. Rather a man's work can provide self-discipline and in many cases a personal satisfaction and growth. The book of Proverbs offers repeated comments of this sort (e.g., 6:6–11; 18:9; 24:30–34), and Paul suggested that idleness breeds irresponsibility not only about self-support but about other things as well (II Thess. 3:6–13). Further, a man's work is a service to other people that should help meet their needs and enrich their lives; in fact, a life of loving service to others is set before us as the Christian ideal. Jesus' example, both as a carpenter and in his public ministry, was dramatized by his washing the disciples' feet; he sets the pattern for work as a contribution to others. Finally, a man's work done wholeheartedly can express his devotion to God and be itself an act of worship (Col. 3:22–4:1). Evidently work—even the "secular"—is a divine calling, so that religious devotion is not confined to the inner life or to those times when we directly address ourselves to God. There should be no dichotomy of secular and sacred. Everything a man does becomes sacred when he does it for the glory of God.

But is it all of *eternal* value? Does the secular endure when this life is over?

Obviously, the physical things we make disintegrate, and we

are told not to spend ourselves for that which perishes. Yet that has to do not so much with *what* we do as with *why* we do it, whether to accumulate treasures on earth or for more ultimate purposes. Plainly, the most mundane task done for the glory of God, or out of love for others, or in such a way that it builds character, has eternal value. In these regards there may be as much eternal value in a Christian's political activity that works to remedy social injustice, or in disciplined study that stretches his mind or struggles to integrate his faith with his learning, or in the business undertaking that enriches the quality of people's lives— "secular" tasks in some people's vocabulary—as there is in quietly cultivating one's own peace of mind, accumulating more Biblical information, or attending religious meetings.

What is it in a man that survives death anyway? It is his personality, replete with his values and beliefs and the qualities of character and mind that he cultivated in this life. Whatever contributes to making a person what he forever will be, then, has eternal significance. We shall take with us more than we sometimes think.

## 5. Sacred and secular learning

Now we must return to the consequences of turning from a sacred-secular disjunction to a more holistic idea of vocation rooted in the doctrine of creation. We have talked of sacred and secular as they apply to all kinds of human activity and involvement in order to remove objections to the unity of truth and to "secular" learning. If the sacred-secular distinction fades and we grant that all truth is ultimately God's truth, then intellectual work can be God's work as much as preaching the gospel, feeding the hungry, or healing the sick. It too is a sacred task. If intellectual work can be God's work and if all truth is God's truth, then we have no reason to denigrate some areas of learning by regarding them either as worldly or as beyond help or as having little or no importance.

On the contrary, such learning needs to be restored to the wholeness of God's truth from which it is torn. It must be thoroughly understood if it is to be properly interpreted, refined, and, where necessary, corrected. All learning is of importance because it bears witness to truth and so to the God of truth.

We find help in seeing how this may be in the work of Herman Dooyeweerd,[2] the Dutch Christian philosopher. He points out that man is at heart a religious being, but that religion is what unifies his life and thought, rather than a limited part of things. Whether a man is a believer or not, he works and acts and thinks out of the religious heart of his being. Since everything is then at heart a religious activity, the secular-sacred distinction disappears. Moreover, because the law of God governs all creation it affects every sphere of human activity and structures every science. Dooyeweerd distinguishes fourteen "law spheres," each with its own structures open to scientific inquiry and all of them unified by their common reference to God and his law. Thus, all nature and all thought bear witness, and the believer finds that his understanding is unified around the Biblical "ground motive" of creation and divine law, as well as sin and grace.

One does not need to agree with all aspects of Dooyeweerd's thought to appreciate the fundamentally Christian character of his vision. He helps us see how the objective divine basis for the unity of truth (metaphysical objectivity)[3] overcomes any sacred-secular distinction, and that there is a personal basis in the heart of man (epistemological subjectivity) for seeing all of learning in relation to God. The basic Biblical distinction is not between sacred and secular but between God and his creation.

The human value of learning is both instrumental and intrinsic. It has instrumental value in that much of what is learned can be "used" in other tasks, both "secular" and more directly "religious." Engineering and architecture are useful in building both houses and churches, music is used for both entertainment and worship, philosophy has a bearing on politics and science as well as on theology and apologetics. But a utilitarian approach is not enough for one who values what God has made. To develop the mind is incumbent upon everyone who values the potential God gave him. To enjoy the arts is important if we value human

---

2. His *magnum opus,* in which the idea of the religious root of theoretical thought and the doctrine of law spheres is worked out in detail, is *A New Critique of Theoretical Thought* in four volumes (Presbyterian & Reformed Publ. Co., 1953). While he stresses divine law without the *Logos* doctrine which we stressed in chapter one, the two are obviously related. A good introduction to his thought may be found in L. Kalsbeek, *Contours of a Christian Philosophy* (Wedge Publ. Co., 1975).

3. See chapter one, where this terminology was introduced.

creativity as part of God's image in man. To understand the sciences is to understand more fully God's handiwork. All this is of intrinsic worth. And truth too is to be valued for itself because all truth is God's and comes from him.

Admittedly, learning like anything else brings temptations. One temptation is to intellectual pride. But the cure for intellectual pride is not ignorance, any more than the cure for sexual license is celibacy. To prize ignorance, when God gives us the capacity and opportunity for understanding, is a sin, just as requiring celibacy is wrong in view of God's call to make marriage something holy. The ultimate cure for sin is the grace of God which can overcome both sexual license and intellectual pride. Moreover, in regard to pride, it is a little knowledge and not a lot that is a dangerous thing. The person who has worked for years to acquire extensive learning usually recognizes how little he knows. The horizons of his knowledge are also the frontiers of his ignorance. But the undisciplined mind that has not learned its own limitations more easily takes selfish pride in the little it knows.

Another temptation inherent in learning is to compromise the truth. Some well-thought-out human ideas are obviously incompatible, taken as they come, with Christian doctrine and ethics. A man can readily fail to see the depth of such conflicts or the complexity of the issues they raise, and he might even adapt his reading of Scripture in deference to current understandings.

This temptation does not arise from learning as such, but from particular ideas and theories that some people hold. The dicta we often hear, ''psychology teaches . . .'' or ''philosophy says . . . ,'' are really meaningless. It is individual psychologists who teach, not psychology *per se;* it is individual philosophers who say things, not philosophy itself. Psychologists do not agree among themselves and neither do philosophers. Psychology is not itself alien to Christianity, nor is philosophy: in fact there have been and are Christian psychologists and philosophers who regard their work as a Christian calling.

We cannot avoid the temptation to error and compromise either by refusing to learn or by bracketing whole areas of inquiry, for then we will more likely err out of ignorance than through knowledge. The remedy for error is more and better understanding, not less. To avoid error requires a disciplined examination of all the alternatives in the light of all the relevant data and arguments and in the light of the Christian revelation. There is no royal road to that kind of learning. We must face error head on and sift it out of the learning we acquire.

The claim that all truth is God's truth thus compels us to inquire more fully what truth is and how error arises. The next two chapters do this in the light of both the Biblical idea of truth and the belief that God gave man the capacity to know. Since others have of course explored these topics, we shall use some of their ideas to help develop our own.

# THREE

# What Is Truth?

Pilate's question is still with us. It was a rhetorical question, occasioned by Jesus' claim to "bear witness to the truth." Perhaps it expressed his cynicism about the perennial religious and political disagreements of Jesus' accusers, rather than voicing a serious inquiry. But his words were spoken out of the divided philosophical background of a Roman culture. On the one hand, Stoics and Platonists dogmatically maintained that truth is unchanging and universal, the same for everyone, that it is rooted in the unchanging rational structure of what is ultimately real, and that while it transcends changing human opinions it is nonetheless accessible to a disciplined logical mind. On the other hand, Sceptics argued that all judgments are relative, all arguments are indecisive, all so-called knowledge is mere opinion, and truth—if indeed there be any that is unchanging and universal—remains utterly unknown.

These two attitudes are still with us today as we saw in the first chapter, on the one hand in the rationalist's demand for objective knowledge with logical demonstration, and on the other in a kind of pragmatic relativism that is satisfied with whatever is immediately relevant or works in the present situation rather than being immutably true. The quiet confidence of Jesus' assertion challenges them both. To the one he talks modestly of bearing witness rather than of rational demonstration, and to the other he speaks as if he already knows the universal truth which men despair of finding.

The idea of witness-bearing deserves closer consideration. Paul claims that God has not left himself without witness in that he gives us rain and fruitful seasons (Acts 14:15–17), as if to echo the Psalmist's witness that "the heavens declare the glory of God" (Ps. 19:1–6). The power of God may be seen in his creation (Rom. 1:19–20), whatever the outcome of our attempts at

objective and logical proofs for his existence. In analogous fashion, John the Baptist came "to bear witness" to the light of the
*Logos* (John 1:6–8), who himself "declared" the Father. Jesus'
claim to witness-bearing should be read against this background.
As the creation attests the creator, as John attests the identity of
the Messiah, so Jesus attests the truth—and the Christian church
in turn attests the grace and truth of God at work in the world
today.

While there is, of course, more to the idea of revelation than
this, witness-bearing is plainly associated with God's self-
revelation in nature, in Christ, and in the church. In other words,
God is known because he reveals himself to men through the
witness of his creatures and his Son. Truth, says Jesus, is similarly known. This is both an impressive and a modest claim:
impressive because it implies that truth is ultimately revealed to
men by God; modest because it suggests that logical demonstration and scientific confirmation may not be necessary to knowing
the truth. The absence of such objective proof does not necessarily lead to scepticism. Somehow the whole creation attests the
truth, and a man can grasp it with all his being (or be grasped by
it) so that he too bears witness. What then is truth, that its revelation captures the minds and hearts of men?[1]

## 1. God and truth

We have already introduced the early Christian claim that all truth
is God's truth wherever it be found. The theist who believes that
God is omniscient thereby affirms that God knows all the truth
about everything and knows it perfectly. As creator of all he is the
ultimate source of all our knowledge, so that our attempts to
know truth are dependent on him and bear tacit witness to him.
As his love and justice are the source and the norm for human
love and justice, so his knowledge is the source and norm for
ours. All truth is thereby God's truth, no matter where it is found.

Two implications immediately follow. (1) The first is that
*truth is not relative but absolute,* that is to say unchanging and
universal. If God's knowledge is complete and perfectly true,

---

1. The question is not about the so-called tests of truth. Chapter seven will
   discuss that subject. We are concerned here not with criteria but with the
   basic nature of truth itself.

then truth itself cannot change; it remains the same for every time and place in creation; it is absolute.

This line of thought is sometimes confused with Plato's philosophy. Realizing that this world is not perfect and unchanging and that our perception of it yields no more than changeable and fallible opinion, Plato pointed to another realm that is unchangeably the same, a transcendent realm of eternal, universal, and ideal forms. For Plato, then, truth is unchanging and universal because it concerns eternal forms rather than particular things and people, and he who loves the truth will turn away from this world to the eternal.

Like the theist, Plato sees truth as unchanging and universal, but he makes it an autonomous universal ideal while the theist sees truth, like everything else, as dependent on God.[2] Moreover, Plato despairs of finding truth revealed in physical and historical things, whereas the theist believes that God has revealed himself in his physical and historical creation: all creation bears witness.

Plato's problem was that since physical objects and events change, our perception of them varies too. It is relative; absolute truth is lacking. But there is nonetheless a sense in which the unchanging nature of truth is reflected even in what we say about changing particulars. In a few months, for instance, my nineteen-year-old son will no longer be nineteen, but it will remain unchangeably true that he was still nineteen on this date. It is not the case in Britain as it is in the United States that cars drive on the right side of the street, but it is unchangeably true that as of this date they do not. Whether you read this in London or New York or Timbuktoo these two truths remain: in that sense they are universally as well as unchangeably true. Some truths then are localized and dated in that they are about a particular place or time, but even so they remain unchangeable and universal in regard to that place and time.[3] Individual truths about changing things are not altogether relative. They bear witness to what is unchanging and so universal.

Individual truths about unchanging things bear even clearer

---

2. Some equate Plato's Idea of the Good with God. Whether or not Plato intended this equation, it hardly yields the one personal, self-revealing creator of Biblical theism.

3. Aristotle therefore defined the law of non-contradiction as applying *at the same time* and *in the same respect,* and in this sense it is a universal and necessary law of logic. See further in chapter six.

witness. Centuries ago, Augustine argued from logical and mathematical truths like $A = A$ or $2 + 2 = 4$ to a universal and unchanging Truth on which such lesser truths depend, a Truth that by definition he identified with God himself. Unchanging truths depend on an unchanging reality, universal truths on a reality that is everywhere the same, and the unity of truth on whatever ultimately unifies all that is real. The only unchanging, universally-the-same, and unifying reality is none other than God himself. His perfect knowledge is the ideal, and he makes possible for men that knowledge of truth which we attain, truth that by its unchanging and universal nature bears witness to Truth as it is in God.[4]

(2) The second implication of the claim that all truth is God's truth is that *truth is inherently personal,* not autonomous like the ideal forms of Plato's *Republic,* nor an abstract ideal to be approached with detachment and "epistemological objectivity" as in Enlightenment epistemology. A look at the terms used in Scripture will open up more fully this connection between the personal and the epistemological.

When Jesus spoke of bearing witness to the truth he spoke of truth in the Biblical manner—personal truth as well as propositional. The Old Testament word for truth (*emeth*) is primarily an ethical rather than an epistemological term. It indicates reliability and fidelity and is used of behavior (Gen. 24:49), of promises (II Sam. 7:28), and of just laws (Neh. 9:13). The Psalmist sees the faithfulness of God in his creation, his mercy, and his justice (Ps. 89). Personal truth is expected of men as well as of God: honesty (Ps. 15:2) and justice (Isa. 59:14–15) are not merely outward qualities but must stem from the heart of a man. Truth is first a matter of inner character and only derivatively a quality of words and deeds.

In the New Testament the idea of fidelity is more often borne by *pistos* (faithful) than by *alēthēs* (true), but John uses a variant of the latter adjective (*alēthinos*) to contrast the "true light" with a less reliable one and the "true bread" with corruptible manna, and to speak of "true worshippers" and the "true vine." The Herodians said to Jesus, "We know that you are true (*alēthēs*),

---

4. See Augustine's *On Free Will,* book II. For a more recent development of a similar line of thought compare William Temple, *Mens Creatrix* (Macmillan, 1949), Part I.

and teach the way of God in truth" (Matt. 22:16)—a clear suggestion of personal fidelity underlying the truth of his teachings.

In the Bible the truth of a proposition is related to the truthfulness of the speaker. What God says is unchangingly true because of his character (e.g. Job 28:20–28). What God says by making us rational beings is also reliable: we have a capacity for knowing. Nor is this capacity destroyed by human sin, for it depends on God more than on us; so Paul declares that men can know something of the truth without being personally truthful (Rom. 1:19–25). The most deluded pagan and the most untrustworthy scoundrel possess fragments of truth and might know a great deal more about many things in God's creation (and even about Christian theology) than the finest saint. Of course he who knows the truth with integrity will obey it (Rom. 1:18), but the possibility of men knowing it at all depends on what thologians call "general revelation" and "common grace."

A similar relation between the truth of propositions and personal truth appears in regard to special revelation. The message of Christ and his apostles is validated by faithful witnesses who speak the truth faithfully (John 5:30–39; 16:13–15). We also speak of the truthfulness or veracity of Scripture, both in the sense that its divine author is personally reliable in what he says (II Tim. 3:14–17), and in the sense that what Scripture teaches is true. Yet the ultimate locus of truth is not just in true propositions, not even in the written statements of Scripture, but in the utter reliability of the true God, one jot or tittle of whose word can never pass away (Matt. 5:17–18). Trust in God implies confidence in the truth of Scripture.

Propositional truth, then, depends on the personal truthfulness of God. To this all our knowledge of anything at all ultimately bears witness, for whatever we learn should remind us of the fidelity as well as the wisdom of the creator. Knowledge too may become not an impersonal accumulation of lifeless facts but an intensely personal involvement, for both the facts we know and the fact that we know at all depend on God. While the Bible views truth as personal, then, it is not "personal" in the sense of being individually relative, but rather in the sense of being a deeply meaningful and even a religious concern.

Jesus Christ not only claimed to teach and to bear witness to the truth: he also claimed to *be* the truth (*alētheia,* John 14:6).

Here too is the idea of God's perfect faithfulness, now revealed in his Son; but it also reminds us of Paul's teaching in Colossians 2 about Christ the creator, "in whom are hid all treasures of wisdom and knowledge." He is the truth, omniscient, to be sure, but also the one who illumines human understanding. As creator and lord of all, his self-revelation brings truth into focus, uncovers the basis of its unity, and reaffirms its universality. To know him is the key to seeing things as a meaningful whole.

A similar account may therefore be given of terms for knowledge as for truth. For the Greek philosophers knowledge is *epistēmē:* the noun form as well as its meaning suggest something abstract, objective, and conclusive. The further term *theōria* suggests the theoretical, or a spectator attitude to life. The Biblical writers prefer the broader terms *ginōskō* and *epiginōskō,* verbs whose action suggests "epistemological subjectivity." They emphasize less the static qualities of objects and more the human act of knowing, be it hearing or seeing, or having moral convictions, or knowing other people, or knowing God. The verb is even used in the Septuagint of marital intercourse: plainly a man does not "know" his wife in a detached, theoretical way, nor is our knowledge of God and his grace detached and theoretical either. To know is to know *for oneself,* to interiorize what is learned, to act on it, to make it one's own. Such knowledge is life-related: it not only affects personality and conduct but is part of life's action. Knowledge, being personal and not detached, brings responsibility: a man must measure up to the truth he knows and behave accordingly, or the very truth he knows condemns him. He must "do the truth" he knows (e.g., I John 1:6,8; 2:4; 3:18–19).[5]

The Biblical concept of wisdom fits the same pattern. Whereas the Greek philosophers distinguished it sharply from *technē* or skill, the Septuagint uses *sophia* of the technical ability of artisans as well as of religious insight and moral conduct. It is a personally enriching and God-given understanding of life's tasks. In the Old Testament poetic books, the man who is not wise is not just ignorant but a fool, and that is a morally culpable state of affairs. Wisdom is always personal: in fact, perfect wisdom is personified in Proverbs 8 as having been with God from all eternity and at the creation, as well as being the divine source of all human wisdom.

---

5. This conception of "doing the truth" is developed by E.J. Carnell in part one of his *Christian Commitment* (Macmillan, 1957).

At the same time a contrast runs through Scripture between two sorts of wisdom: the one coming from God is true and reliable, the other is deceptive and false. The book of Ecclesiastes poses a tension between two faces of wisdom—the one unaware of its divine source and so humanly unsatisfying, the other consciously dependent on the creator and bringing enrichment to life. I Corinthians 1-2 contrasts the wisdom of God and the wisdom of this world, while the Colossian epistle, as we saw in chapter one, presents a conflict of world-views.

In no place does Scripture deprecate the love of wisdom or the pursuit of truth. The "wisdom of the world" is not human knowledge *per se,* nor is it knowledge about the natural world; man's knowledge of nature is knowledge about God's creation, a witness-bearing knowledge that is neither vain nor foolish. Rather, the key to the I Corinthians passage is the Old Testament account of the fool who excludes God from his life; in this context he excludes God's saving work in Christ and tries to know God independently of the cross. But if all truth and wisdom depend ultimately on the personal fidelity of a self-revealing God, then the world that leaves God out is really not wise at all, but foolish.

To summarize the implications of relating truth to God:

(1) To say that truth is absolute rather than relative means that it is unchanging and universally the same.

(2) Truth is absolute not in or of itself but because it derives ultimately from the one, eternal God. It is grounded in his "metaphysical objectivity," and that of his creation.

(3) Absolute propositional truth, therefore, depends on the absolute personal truth (or fidelity) of God, who can be trusted in all he does and says.

(4) All knowledge ultimately bears witness to the truth God reveals. Both the intelligibility of nature and the cognitive powers of man attest God's fidelity.

(5) The propositional truth of the Biblical revelation likewise depends on and bears witness to the personal fidelity of God, and the ultimate unity of truth is specially revealed in Jesus Christ.

(6) Human knowledge is, therefore, not detached and purely theoretical but intensely personal. Because truth captures the hearts and minds of men, it admits of "epistemological

subjectivity.'' Because knowledge depends on God's fidelity, the believer's pursuit of knowledge can express his trust in God.

Of these conclusions, (1) is denied by the relativist and sceptic. (2) and (3) and (4) are denied not only by the relativist or sceptic but also by the rationalist who makes truth autonomous and self-sustaining in its universality. The rationalist and the sceptic also forget (6), for they regard human knowledge as purely objective and theoretical, as if it can be detached from our larger personal involvements and responsibilities, whether moral or religious or whatever. They separate the personal from the epistemological.

We shall now look at these conclusions in past attempts to relate truth to God; this historical glimpse will show how propositional and personal truth came to be separated, how therefore we lost the religious unity of truth. It will also show some efforts to reunite them.

## 2. Augustine and medieval concepts of truth

Christian philosophers of the Middle Ages from Augustine to Duns Scotus attempted to develop a Christian view of truth with the help of the Greek theory of universal forms. According to Plato, truth is universal and unchanging because the reality to which it pertains is not the changing world of physical particulars but a transcendent and autonomous realm of universal and unchanging ideals that somehow determines the essential nature of the physical world. Human knowledge is knowledge of these archetypes, and will therefore provide unchanging truth that is universally the same. Aristotle and Plotinus somewhat modified the scheme, but they retained the basic view that truth is absolute because what we know is the universal and unchanging form of things rather than changing particulars.

It was this view which Augustine and others tried to convert to Christianity. That it needs conversion is obvious, for it lacks any doctrine of *ex nihilo* creation,[6] and it regards universal and eternal

---

6. *ex nihilo* (out of nothing) contrasts absolute creation with one that organizes uncreated matter (as in Plato and dualistic philosophies), or that emanates from the eternal being of God (as with Plotinus' pantheism). With *ex nihilo* creation, everything that exists is either God himself or else depends on God for its very existence. Nothing is independent of him or autonomous.

truths (*rationes aeternae*) as an impersonal and self-sustaining realm of being. Plato and Plotinus conceived of a One, and Aristotle an Unmoved Mover, that coordinates and unifies all the eternal forms, but in neither case does absolute truth depend on a personal and ethical deity who creates out of nothing. Augustine therefore modified the Greek view by identifying the archetypes (*rationes aeternae*) with the eternal counsels and decrees of God so that, instead of being autonomous, truth now depends on the unchanging wisdom of God. All truth about everything that is or could be is known eternally to God and depends on the trustworthiness of his eternal wisdom and decrees. In company with earlier church fathers, Augustine regarded the eternal *Logos* as the personal embodiment of that eternal wisdom.

But God is the creator who makes everything "after its kind." He made what he created orderly and intelligible by implanting forms in matter, as seminal deposits (*rationes seminales*) of the eternal archetypes. Our knowledge of physical particulars is thus a knowledge of God's wisdom there displayed. In the case of man, a changeless form is divinely implanted in his body to shape his life; it is human reason and constitutes his immortal soul. Human reason is the image of God in man, for it reflects in its knowledge the eternal wisdom of God. Augustine understands this to mean that the divine *Logos* enlightens every man with innate truths about God, morals, and reason itself. These *rationes aeternae* in the soul of man provide us with unchanging and universal truth, and Christ the truth is the teacher within. Augustine thereby reaches conclusions (1), (2), and (4).

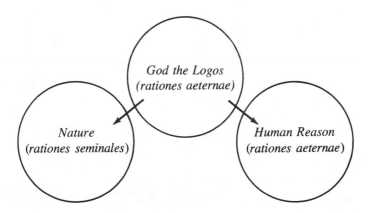

Even though he does not explicitly discuss conclusion (3), the dependence of propositional truth on personal truth or fidelity, Augustine has clearly rooted propositional truth in the unchanging wisdom of a personal God. This relationship entices him to go beyond conclusion (4), the *witness* of knowledge to God, and to *argue* as we indicated previously for the existence of God. He contends that unchanging truths about mathematics and logic are known by all men, even when they doubt them, and he points out that these truths are superior to our thinking, for our thinking does not make them true but rather is judged by them. Truth must then derive from something superior to the human mind, from the source of truth that embraces all truths in its unity. Such a Truth must therefore exist, and by definition this is God. The argument is an early version of the famous "ontological proof" for the existence of God. It depends on Augustine's theory of innate knowledge (*rationes aeternae*), and on the theory of forms. But if it therefore fails as a theistic argument, it does not fail to note the witness of our knowledge to God.

When it comes to conclusion (6), the personal character of human knowledge, Augustine is more clear-sighted. He rejects the classical view that man's rationality is so autonomous that he can rule his life by reason alone, because he saw the human person more as a unified whole than as a collection of discrete parts. Neither our beliefs nor our moral and political lives are governed by reason alone; a man is ruled not by what he knows but by what he most loves as a whole person and with his whole heart. Knowledge is tied to our personal involvements: it is not impersonal nor detached.

A similar view of truth appears later in Anselm. In addition to speaking of archetypal truths in the mind of God and of the truth of propositions, he discusses "truth in the will," or personal truthfulness. In the writings of Thomas Aquinas, similarly, we read of archetypal truths in the divine *Logos,* of seminal forms that give particular things their intelligible nature, and of truth as the "adequation" of thought to the things we claim to know, so that once again all truth depends on a personal God who makes nature intelligible and gives man his rational soul.

But Aquinas tends to overlook conclusions (3) and (6), the personal side of truth: while the propositional truth men gain depends on the wisdom of the Creator, it is not overtly related to his personal truthfulness. Similarly, Aquinas finds human reason sufficiently independent of the moral will to proceed in a detached and objective fashion. The image of God in man is the intellect, which remains unsullied by our loss of moral likeness to God through sin; our knowledge of universal truths about nature and man, and of what we can deduce with regard to God and morality, remains intact. Sin may affect our willingness to act on what we know, but not our knowledge as such.

As a result, Aquinas has been criticized as a rationalist who makes reason autonomous and theoretical rather than a fully personal activity affected by man's moral and religious condition. Duns Scotus tried to remedy this by stressing the voluntary aspects of knowing and the sovereign freedom of God in his creative and legislative work. But it involved a radical change in the Greek theory of universal forms and contributed to the abandonment of that theory altogether.

Christian philosophers are still divided as to the legitimacy and effectivenss of the medieval attempt at a synthesis of Christianity with Greek thought, but it was plainly a far-sighted endeavor to preserve both the dependence of truth on God and the fully personal character of human knowledge. Aquinas preserved the first part of this vision but compromised the second, and the autonomy of human reason was his legacy to the modern mind.

### 3. Descartes and Enlightenment rationalism

With the decline of the Greek theory of forms, a new approach to the nature of truth was needed. René Descartes (d. 1650) provided this approach in the correspondence theory of truth that ruled European philosophy for centuries and is still widely held today. To understand it we must first recognize the influence of mechanistic science with its mathematical account of the laws of nature and the movements of physical bodies. Descartes and his successors idolized mathematical reasoning as the pattern for all human knowledge: beginning with universally true axioms, they hoped to deduce a whole systematic structure of conclusions that are themselves unchangingly and universally true.

That thinking of this sort is purely theoretical and detached from the fuller life of the human person is dramatically evident in Descartes' own procedure. Shutting himself up in a stove-heated room for some winter weeks, he methodically suspended judgment on everything he could conceivably doubt—including the reality of his own shivering body and the cold world outside—until out of his universal doubt one indubitable truth distilled. *Dubito, ergo sum:* I doubt, therefore I exist, a thinking thing, whether or not I have a body and whether or not anything else exists at all. The conscious intellect is therefore autonomous, independent of all bodily and personal involvements.

Descartes remains a theist and sees clearly the dependence of truth on God. At first he hypothesizes that some malign demon may be deceiving us into taking as true what actually is false, and he is unable to lay to rest the possibility of reason deluding him until he knows that God exists. But if such a perfect being exists, it would be self-contradictory for him to deceive. Nor could he give me rational ability "of such a sort that I could ever go wrong when I use it properly." Consequently, not only the truth itself but also our capacity for knowing the truth depends on the personal truthfulness of God, whose words and deeds alike can never lie. Error does not depend on God but stems from man's abuse of his capacity for truth.[7]

In effect, then, Descartes takes his place as a Christian thinker by resting cognitive truth on the personal truth of God, and laying the blame for error not on God and his works but on the exercise of the human will. To involve the will as well as the intellect in knowing the truth is something he undoubtedly learned from previous Christian philosophers, whether Augustine or Duns Scotus or whomever, and it makes knowledge more personal than if it involved the intellect alone.

But it was not enough. Separating the faculties of will and intellect divides the person, and Descartes interprets his further division between mind and body to mean that it is the mind alone rather than the whole person who knows. In fact, he argued, I know that I exist and that God exists, and I know the essential nature of material things, without even knowing whether I have a material body or whether any material things exist at all. My ideas and knowledge are in my mind and I only know that anything else exists—God or other minds or a material world—if I can prove it from the content and existence of my mind and its ideas. And since all I have to start with is my mind and its ideas, I can be quite detached and objective about it all.

The result is that truth pertains to the ideas and judgments of

---

7. *Meditations on First Philosophy,* Fourth Meditation. More will be said about human error in chapter four.

the mind and consists in the correspondence of those ideas to the realities they represent.[8] Reason becomes in all its activities just what it is in mathematics: autonomous (self-governing), sovereign (so that man and society live under "the rule of reason"), objective, and theoretical. This races far beyond the modesty of "bearing witness" to the truth, and loses the more fully personal nature of knowledge and truth.

Descartes' successors gradually lost his reliance for truth on the fidelity of a personal God. George Berkeley retains it by tracing directly to God all the ideas we receive from outside the mind, and Leibniz by making each mind mirror eternal truths in the mind of God. But many Enlightenment thinkers, and many empiricists today who share some of Descartes' rational ideals or the correspondence theory of truth, talk of truth independently of God as if it were a self-sustaining ideal and as if human reason were a purely objective and impersonal activity. Descartes' failure was not in the relation he saw of truth to God, but in the lack of relation he saw between man's rational capacity for knowing truth and his personality as a whole. Conclusion (6) is missing.

## 4. Kierkegaard and personal truth

The ensuing reaction against Enlightenment rationalism had both good and bad effects. On the negative side was a tendency to subordinate reason to emotion: Wordsworth's early poetry, for example, was vigorously anti-intellectual and the overall Romantic movement contributed in that direction. By rejecting the orthodox doctrine of creation *ex nihilo* and regarding God as immanent within nature, Romanticism made both nature and man ultimately divine and so lost any basis for absolute truth in a personal creator who transcends the changing world. The result was relativism about religious truth (hence the liberal theology that grew from Schleiermacher's romanticism) and relativism in ethics.

On the positive side, the reaction against Enlightenment rationalism produced a richer view of man and his relationship to truth. One important representative is Søren Kierkegaard, the so-called father of modern existentialism. Theologically he was an orthodox Lutheran who emphasized the transcendence of the

---

8. Descartes seems to *define* truth as correspondence but he advances an intuitive *test* for truth: we recognize true ideas when their overwhelming clarity and distinctness puts them beyond doubt.

eternal God and the incarnation of God in the historical Jesus
Christ, and who acknowledged the divine authority and truth of
Scripture. Consequently, Kierkegaard's concern is less about the
divine source of truth, which he acknowledged without difficulty,
and more about how men are to approach the truth. In his *Concluding Unscientific Postscript* he distinguishes two ways: the
objective and the subjective. The objective is characteristic of
rationalism: Kierkegaard's examples are speculative philosophy
with its theoretical proofs for the existence of God, and the historical approach that amasses endless evidence concerning the origins of Christianity and the authenticity of its Scriptures. But
while Christian doctrine is objectively true ("metaphysical objectivity"), Christian faith is far more than a set of objectively held
propositions ("epistemological objectivity"). It is an inner faith
of such a passionately personal sort that a qualitative gap remains
between any purely objective approach to the propositional truth
of Christian doctrine on the one hand, and the subjective approach to Christianity on the other.

Kierkegaard's subjective path is wholly personal. "Subjectivity" does not mean "it's all in your mind," any more than
"personal" means it is individually relative. "Subject-hood"
would be a better term: the subjective path involves the man as a
subject who doubts and hopes and believes and loves and dreads
with all his heart and all the intensity of his being, not just his
intellect with its reasoning powers. By the subjective path a man
approaches truth passionately, not detachedly, and his response
to truth is an outburst of wholehearted faith. When he knows the
truth this way, personally, he knows it in the Biblical sense of
knowing: he is *in* the truth and he obeys it from the heart.

Kierkegaard returns us, then, to where Christian thought began. Other existentialists share his rejection of the Enlightenment
view: some retain the theistic basis of truth and some do not, but
all retain the insistence that truly human knowledge must be fully
personal if it is to be relevant to a unified human existence.

Other twentieth century revolts against the Enlightenment
point in parallel directions, though not as clearly. William
James,[9] for instance, maintains that when rational arguments and

---

9. See especially his essays "The Sentiment of Rationality," "The Will to
   Believe," and "Pragmatism's Conception of Truth" in *Essays in Pragmatism* (Hafner Publ. Co., 1948).

empirical evidence fail to settle a dispute, and we are forced to choose between momentous and live options, then we rightfully decide on the basis of what will satisfy the other demands human nature makes on what we believe or do. But James failed to ground truth in God, and consequently he speaks of truth as if it were relative to changing situations. Not surprisingly, pragmatism has contributed to the development of ethical relativism, including recent situation ethics.

A further example is the work of Michael Polanyi, the distinguished British philosopher of science.[10] While insisting that our knowledge lays claim to universal truth (he prefers the term "validity"), he reminds us that to purport to know is a responsible *personal* act, an intellectual commitment. Knowledge is objective in the sense of having contact with objective reality ("metaphysical objectivity"), but it is also personal in various ways. The scientist values simplicity and symmetry and economy in a theory, his science depends on his skill and insight, and he is forever called on to judge the sufficiency of evidence. He only transcends what is relative to his intellectual values and skills and judgments by striving wholeheartedly to fulfil his personal obligation to universal standards. Consequently, Polanyi repudiates the ideal of knowledge as wholly dispassionate and dominated completely by objective and empirical evidence ("epistemological objectivity").

The examples could be multiplied, but one more must suffice. The Dutch philosopher Herman Dooyeweerd,[11] whose influence on some strains of evangelical and reformed thought is profound, goes to great length to reject the autonomy of reason and the self-sufficiency of truth. Since truth is rooted in the transcendent creator, a man's grasp of the proper unity of truth depends on whether he is also himself inwardly rooted in God. Just as the Christian idea of truth is holistic and should "permeate scientific thought from root to crown," so too it affects our full selfhood from the religious heart of our existence outward into all of life and thought. This idea of truth embraces both our subjecthood and our objectivity.

---

10. Especially his *Personal Knowledge* (Harper, 1964) and *The Tacit Dimension* (Doubleday, 1966).
11. See *In the Twilight of Western Thought* (Presbyterian & Reformed Publ. Co., 1960); also *A New Critique of Theoretical Thought*, vol. II, pp. 549–598.

The conception of personal truth which has thus reemerged in twentieth century thought faces major problems. First, if it is detached from the personal and transcendent creator, it lapses into something purely humanistic and potentially relative. Second, by virtue of the whole person's involvement with truth, the role of reason and the place of propositional truth need to be clearly delineated. One example of the failure to do this is the way Emil Brunner distinguishes between it-truth and thou-truth, the former propositional and the latter personal.[12] I know a person truly though an interpersonal encounter (I-Thou relationship), but whenever I try to state objectively what he truly is and how he revealed himself to me, then I falsify the truth. Brunner applies his disjunction of the propositional and the personal to the concept of divine revelation: God's self-revelation to men has the character of an I-Thou encounter, the personal character of which is lost—both my personal involvement with God and his person-as-revealed—when I try to state what God is like or the meaning of what he has done. Consequently Scripture, being a written statement about God's Word and acts, is a purely human witness to God's self-revelation and not itself God's revelation. Propositional revelation is impossible.

Enough has been written on this subject to make an extensive rejoinder unnecessary here.[13] In effect Brunner forgets that subjective and objective attitudes are not wholly separate but represent rather the two poles of a gradation of attitudes. Pure subjectivity would be an utter absorption devoid of reflection, and it does not occur in human persons except perhaps in a hypnotic or mystic or psychedelic state. Likewise, pure objectivity does not occur, for personal interest and judgments intrude even into scientific thought. Rather, there is some objectivity in all our subjectivity, and some subjectivity in all our objectivity, in varying

---

12. See *Truth as Encounter* (Westminster, 1964). Brunner applies to theology the "I-Thou" notion developed by Martin Buber: see *I and Thou* (Scribner's, 1958).

13. In particular see William Hordern, *Speaking of God* (Macmillan, 1965), and A.F. Holmes, *Faith Seeks Understanding* (Eerdmans, 1971), chapters five and six, esp. pp. 150–162. An alternative relation between the personal and the cognitive, that regards knowing as itself a personal act, is suggested by John Macmurray, *The Self as Agent* (Faber & Faber, 1957) and applied to theology by Robert Blaikie, *"Secular Christianity" and the God Who Acts* (Eerdmans, 1970). Polanyi's influence may be seen in Jerry Gill, *The Possibility of Religious Knowledge* (Eerdmans, 1971).

degrees. In speaking of human relations, for instance, we make use not only of I-thou language and I-it language but also of I-she or I-he. I speak of my wife in such a personal way that when you meet her you realize that you already know her through what I have said. Propositions about a person can and do reveal her true nature. If that were not so, the world of literature would be impersonal, its characters would not "live," and it could reveal nothing of human nature. Brunner needs to be reminded that the language of the Bible is more like the language of literature than that of science, and that such language can and does reveal the nature of persons. Personal truth cannot be separated from the propositional.

One further observation flows from this interrelatedness of personal and propositional truth in God and in man. Some writers regard post-Kantian thought, and especially thinkers like Kierkegaard, the existentialists, and the language analysts, as leading us away from a Christian epistemology. This negative view has lately been popularized in Christian circles by Francis Schaeffer's claim, in *Escape from Reason* and other of his writings, that Kant and Kierkegaard and existentialism have abandoned the rational approach to truth and sunk into irrationalism and relativism. A "line of despair" emerges after Kant, despair about both reason and the meaning of life. Admittedly, Schaeffer is imprecise in his use of terms like "reason": he does not clearly distinguish between reason as *understanding* and reason as *proving* universally true propositions. The former of course is essential to any Christian view of reason, but not necessarily the latter. Yet the kind of reason from which modern man has escaped following Kant and Kierkegaard is more the latter than the former. Not all post-Kantian or even existential thought despairs of intelligible meaning the way Sartre has done. Schaeffer seems not to recognize this distinction. He fails to distinguish the two meanings of objectivity and subjectivity which, we have argued, the Enlightenment missed and more recent thought has recovered. He thereby fails to see clearly how metaphysical objectivity may be combined with epistemological subjectivity. To that extent, his return to reason is as much an echo of Enlightenment rationalism as a renewal of Biblical insight.

My diagnosis is different. The Enlightenment fails, if not to root truth in a personal God, at least to grasp the relation of the human person as a whole to truth, leaving us with both impersonal and impossible demands for objectivity and theoretical proof. Much recent philosophy has moved back from this rationalism to a more fully personal view of knowledge and truth. Sometimes it has swung all the way to the other extreme of relativism, and often it has lost the theistic basis for truth, but at least it has begun to see the essentially personal nature of knowledge and truth which the Scriptures contributed to earlier Western thought. The solution to existential despair and to theological and ethical relativism is not to be found in a return to the rationalism that failed us before, but in advancing to a fuller and more Biblical understanding of the interdependence of personal and propositional truth.

We shall now develop this theme in relation to the problem of error, and then in chapter five relate it to revelation and to faith, in chapter six to the nature of human reasoning, and in chapter seven to the justification of belief.

# FOUR

# All Those Errors!

Human error haunts man's quest for truth as relentlessly as sin and finiteness attend his search for justice and compassion. Error creeps into our moral and political judgments, our theology, our history, our science, our philosophy, and even our reading of other people. It spreads such uncertainty in the path of knowledge that some people despair of finding the truth at all and relapse into scepticism, or satisfy themselves with mystical experience, or else they resort to an unreasoning dogmatism about the faith. We shall say more later about mysticism and dogmatism, and about the means at our disposal for laying the ghost of scepticism to rest and for distinguishing truth from error. The present chapter suggests how error arises, and why, and proposes that it in no way invalidates the quest for truth.

Error is like evil. As evil is to good, so error is to truth. It is a negative feature, a violation or a failure. Philosophers often speak of evil as a privation of the good: error is analogously a privation of the true. Error is in fact a form of evil. It is cognitive evil: the good which the understanding seeks is truth, and the evil it struggles to avoid is error. The problem of error, then, may be approached in similar terms to the problem of evil.

The problem of evil is twofold: first, the theoretical problem of explaining how it can occur in God's creation if God is all-good, all-wise, and all-powerful; second, the more practical problem of restraining it, of avoiding it altogether when possible, and when it occurs of overcoming it with good. Likewise, with regard to error the problem is twofold: first, to explain how it can occur if God is trustworthy in giving us minds to think with and in providing adequate sources of knowledge; and second, to limit and if possible avoid error, and when it occurs to move beyond the error towards a better understanding of the truth.

## 1. Sin and unbelief

One ready response to the problem of evil is to blame it all on man's sin and unbelief, so that sickness and natural disasters as well as war, crime, economic problems, broken homes, and sexual perversions are all the direct consequence of disobeying God. There is precedent in the Old Testament prophets for pointing out moral and religious causes of social problems and national crises, and we are just beginning to appreciate how a global ecological balance can be upset by misusing one resource. So man's fall into sin may well have the wide consequences this response assumes, whether or not they flow as directly from current sins as it often claims.

The same kind of blanket statement is made regarding error: man's unbelief is to blame. The Bible says that Satan has blinded the minds of unbelievers, that the natural man cannot understand, that men refuse to retain God in their knowledge, that the Spirit of God must teach a man if he is to know the truth (I Cor. 1:18–2:14; II Cor. 4:1–6; Rom. 1:19–32). Jesus himself told some Jews who had difficulty with what he taught that their problem was not with his teaching but with their lack of integrity and their unwillingness to receive it. To use the terms we introduced previously, their lack of personal truth prevented them from grasping propositioned truth apart from some special work of the Holy Spirit (John 7:15–18; cp. 8:39–47; 16:12–15). Does this then mean that no truth whatsoever is accessible to unregenerate men, and that they are bound to err apart from some special revelation from God? Is the depravity of human understanding really that total?

Even a cursory examination of the Biblical passages we cited reveals that they are not speaking of the arts and sciences but of a man's ability to discover independently what the Christian revelation uniquely declares, to admit its truth and to commit oneself accordingly to God. They speak of truth and error regarding Jesus Christ and his gospel, not of other kinds of knowledge. Yet if truth is one, are not other matters connected? Will not a man's understanding of other things suffer from his unbelief? Some of the church fathers, we have noted, claim that pagan knowledge is fragmentary, torn from the full context of God's truth. Since pagans do not understand how their knowledge ties together as a whole in relation to the true God, they may indeed as a result distort the fragments; yet they still grasp truth in part, though imperfectly. All truth is God's truth, even when it is fragmentarily and imperfectly known.

Reformed writers like Herman Dooyeweerd and Cornelius Van Til regard the basic difference between believing and apostate thought, or the regenerate and unregenerate mind, as basic to everything else. Dooyeweerd points out that believing thought is rooted in the Biblical "ground-motive" of creation, sin, and grace, and that this root differentiates radically the whole structure of Christian theoretical understanding from that of apostate thought, whose ground-motives are drawn from pagan Greek sources or from some compromising synthesis of Greek and Christian ideas or from modern rationalism or the like. Undoubtedly, this basic difference accounts for much of the error that has crept into Western philosophy and theology and other theoretical sciences. But when all is said and done, is it a sufficient explanation of all disagreement and error? We can hardly reduce disagreements born of misunderstanding and errors born of ignorance to the fruit of unbelief. Neither Dooyeweerd nor Van Til intend anything that simplistic, nor do they imply that devout and informed believers never make mistakes. Moreover, the Biblical ground-motive and other Biblical ideas have had a considerable influence on non-Christian as well as Christian thought, and for this reason also we find fragments and degrees of truth in all sorts of surprising places.

In practice not all matters are equally closely related to the central issues of Christian belief or unbelief. Mathematics is more remote than political science, political science than ethics, and ethics than theology. Within each of these disciplines, likewise, there are degrees of proximity to central issues, so that the choice between an ethic of obligation (usually called "deontological") and a purely utilitarian ethic is more directly related to theism and therefore more crucial than the choice between a formalist and an intuitionist philosophy of mathematics; and the moral reasoning that balances duty with utility in ethics is itself less crucial to Christian concerns than is the fact of man's moral accountability to God. In theology, the full deity and humanity of Jesus Christ is central to the faith, whereas different views of ecclesiastical order are secondary. It follows then that unbelief, addressed as it is to the central tenets of the faith, is likely to have a greater degree of influence on more closely related matters and a lesser influence on more remote items. In fact, it is common experience that the believer has less difficulty learning mathematics from non-Christians than he does political science; he often has less disagreement with them in political science than in ethical theory; and less in ethics than in theology. Yet when he comes in political philosophy to questions about the nature of man and what can prevent man's inhumanity to men, or in ethical theory to man's supposed ability to rule his passions with reason alone, then theological issues are raised and disagreement is likely to remain.

Other problems confront the blanket response that all error is due to personal sin. Many a person has honest problems about the truth of Christianity. He is willing to look into the matter, he has listened carefully to Christian teaching, and no evident moral problems divert his attention; yet in the face of the problem of evil or historical problems about the Biblical record he honestly cannot see that the Christian message is true. What evidence do we have in such a case that unwillingness is wholly to blame? His difficulty has more to do with his limited access to evidence and arguments than with moral turpitude or willful rebellion against God.

Consider also the disagreements that divide informed and upright believers. We hold widely differing political views and even ethical theories. We run the gamut of opinion in such sciences as psychology. And what of theology? Are we to ascribe our lack of unanimity about predestination, baptism, or church government to sin in the church? On many such particulars Christianity is and has been since its early years theologically pluralistic. In some regards our differences may be negotiable and our various views may turn out to be parts of a larger whole. But in other regards the differences are antithetical, as when pedobaptists insist that infant children of covenant families should be baptized while anabaptists deny any such covenant and confine baptism to individual adult believers. In such a case, when each side takes a dogmatic stance that specifically excludes the other, both cannot be wholly right. It seems that the Scriptures may not be as definitive as they suppose, and that misinformation or misunderstanding on at least one side must be in part to blame.

The point is that just as in the problem of evil we identify both moral causes and natural causes, and thereby distinguish moral evils like crime and war from natural evils like earthquakes and cancers, so in the problem of error we must distinguish the moral causes of error from its natural causes. Sin and unbelief are involved at least in some human error, to be sure, but we must also take account of the natural effects of human finiteness.

## 2. Finiteness and free will

Human finiteness becomes evident in a variety of ways. The scope of our past experience, and of all possible human experience, is so limited that we risk error whenever we generalize and whenever we extrapolate from experiences we have had to experiences we anticipate. Our understanding of what we experience is also finite, whether of its causes or of its value or of its ultimate purpose or of what it says of the nature of man and his world. Our judgments are fallible; memory is fallible; even more so is our anticipation of the future. Our mental concentration is limited, and this can keep us from mastering information, following complex arguments, or effectively analyzing a maze of data. We tire, attention wanders, interest lags; we simply cannot give ourselves intellectually to everything, and even if we could we would do so far too superficially.

One element of human finiteness is our temporality. The past glides away, most of it unregistered and beyond recall, while the hidden future and emerging present draw our attention from what we might retain of the past; and no sooner do we seem to grasp the present than it too is past and gone. In addition to our individual temporality we are corporately subject to history. Past history helps shape our knowledge, it informs us, creates a mindset, establishes powerful precedents and intellectual traditions. What our arts and sciences are, and our theology, they are in part because of the successes and failures of a past over which we now have no control. At best we pick up where history places us, accept what we are taught and perhaps sift some of it out, but in any case we build on what is left. This is true of the sciences, of philosophy and theology, and even of the artist's creative work and his perception of life. Our history, along with other aspects of our finiteness, contributes to our errors.

Nor is the Bible an easy panacea. It does not offset all our finiteness, nor was it ever intended to do so, for it is not an exhaustive revelation on all things but a sufficient revelation of what is essential for faith and practice. It is not a scientific source book and it falls short of completeness even on topics that theologians discuss. Its purpose is not encyclopedic but redemptive. It confronts us as finite beings and leaves us still finite, better informed about God's creative and redeeming work to be sure, but still fallible and often in error. We err in matters on which the Bible is silent, but we also err in matters on which it speaks; we may fail to read it aright or may read into it what is not there, for every document is subject to interpretation.

Does the fact that finiteness causes error mean that God bungled his creative work and that he too has erred? If this were so, then our quest for truth would be hopeless, for God would not be wholly trustworthy and we could not rest the hope for propositional truth on the personal truth of God. The theistic basis of truth would disintegrate and our epistemological confidence would be destroyed.

The key to the problem of finiteness and error is that God, in creating us as finite beings, intended that we learn to live with both the possibility and the actual experience of error. He did not make us to be either infallible or omniscient, but to be fallible and limited in our knowledge. We have to accept finiteness and fallibility with our creatureliness and adopt a stance about knowledge that is at the same time properly modest and duly confident. Now we see through a glass darkly, but we still see. Now we know in part, but we can still know.

René Descartes faced this issue squarely in his famous *Meditations*. Starting from the realization that human fallibility and error may leave him sceptical of knowing anything at all, he adopts a method calculated to help him live with fallibility through avoiding error. But it is not until he has established that God exists, wholly perfect in every regard, that in his Fourth Meditation he can handle the problem of error to his satisfaction. Being perfect, God could not deceive us by giving unreliable rational powers while making us think them reliable. That would be a fraud of which he is incapable. God is not the cause of error, nor are my God-given faculties themselves deceptive. I cannot blame God. As God allows man to sin without causing his sin and being to blame, so God allows man to err without causing his error and being to blame for that.

How then can error be explained? First, we must remember that error, like evil, is a defect and a privation. Therefore, it is not necessary that our faculties be specifically designed to err, but only that our power of discerning truth from error be finite. Finiteness means that privation is possible.

Second, Descartes reasons that, being all-powerful, God could have made us incapable of error, yet being perfect he always wills and does what is best. So in God's eyes it is better that we be capable of error than otherwise. Why this is so Descartes cannot say, for he has no way of knowing such purposes of God as have not been revealed. Like Job wrestling with the problem of evil, he rests his case on the personal fidelity of God.

Third, upon closer scrutiny Descartes observes that human error depends on the interplay of two faculties, the understanding and the will. The understanding alone makes no judgments, either true or false, but apprehends the ideas that make up our judgments. To have no idea of something is another kind of privation: it is ignorance, not error. The understanding can be ignorant but it cannot itself err. It can entertain a judgment, but it is the will which affirms or denies it and thereby makes the judgment that is either true or false.

Error, then, springs neither from the understanding alone nor from the will alone, as if God had given us defective faculties, but from an improper act of the will in relation to the intellect. The intellect is finite and has limits; it is sometimes ignorant or unclear. The will is not thus limited but is free to make assertions about things we do not understand. The intellect is tied to what it understands, but the will is free to range beyond. I err when instead of restraining free will within the range of my finite understanding and withholding judgment outside, I allow it full rein without the rule of reason. Then "it readily falls into error and sin by choosing the false in room of the true, and evil instead of good."

Descartes' "free will explanation" of error parallels traditional Christian accounts of evil, and he extends it in his Sixth Meditation to perceptual error, which likewise stems from the wrong *use* of free will and not from a faulty faculty received from God. Error is in no way inconsistent with the personal integrity of the creator, nor with the claim that propositional truth depends on the personal truthfulness of God. Descartes concludes his *Meditations* by confessing that we must "acknowledge the weakness of our nature."

His account is not without difficulties, any more than is the free will explanation of evil. He admits, for example, that pragmatic necessities may force a decision before the understanding has time to satisfy itself, as if life constrains us to err. Either he must admit that life itself is distorted from its original form that it should do this to us, which would force him into a more extended account of natural evil than he gives; or he must allow man to decide pragmatically and provisionally while suspending final judgment, which would force him to modify his overall epistemology along more pragmatic lines; or he must allow that God did not create things as immediately understandable as he supposes, and try to justify this way of God to men. I suspect all three of these paths are ultimately required.

Underlying this difficulty is the realization that just as some evils cannot be traced to human sin and unbelief but are due to natural phenomena, so some error cannot be blamed entirely on free acts of the will but is more due to other natural conditions. The conditions for error, even the virtual unavoidability of error, seem to be inherent in the demands that the present order of creation makes on us. Error is one of the natural evils we have to live with; it is not only a moral evil.

It does not help to blame human error on Satan. The Biblical accounts of evil and of error both acknowledge some Satanic activity, but that is neither the only nor the ultimate explanation. We cannot blame our finiteness on Satan, nor, therefore, our fallibility and all our mistakes. Moreover, just as the sovereign God allowed Satan to try Job, so he allows him to deceive men in whatever regards he does. The conclusion therefore remains: not *all* natural error is attributable to demonic power. And the question remains: why does God permit error?

### 3. Provisional judgments

The strength of Descartes' account is as an analogue to the Christian account of evil and in its ultimate dependence on the personal truthfulness of God. Its weakness is the incompleteness of his "free will explanation," and his failure to see that God might with integrity have made it far more difficult than he supposes for us to avoid error, in some cases even impossible to do so.

Descartes offers us only two ways of avoiding error. The first is to ensure clarity and distinctness of understanding before making a judgment; but things may be so obscure or complex that no one clear understanding is self-evident. Disagreement and error may therefore still arise. The second way is accordingly to withhold judgment; but life and thought may demand of us judgment and action when we have insufficient basis for the unerring finality he desires. In such cases, in fact I think in most cases of human judgment, we can at best offer progress reports or make provisional decisions with degrees of tentativeness proportionate to the degree of understanding and evidence. I affirm that my pen is eight inches long when I am asked, much more tentatively than I affirm it to be black, because I know clearly that it is black but I am only estimating its length. In theology I affirm the deity of Christ with considerably more finality than I affirm my beliefs on church government, because the one has much more Biblical basis than the other and is far more crucial to my understanding of the Christian faith as a whole. But Descartes does not seem to allow us such qualified judgments.

That provisional judgments are often required seems perfectly evident. The demands of teaching and conversation and action are such that we constantly have to say "what we think" about something and why. Approximation, probability, plausibility, hypothesis, sufficient evidence, and openness to correction— these are standard fare in both the sciences and the humanities. Life will not always wait for us to be absolutely certain beyond all further question and discussion: practical matters are often too pressing. Thought itself will not wait either, for in order to explore many an issue we need to adopt a working hypothesis or make other provisional judgments. The difference in evidence between a tentative hypothesis and an established theory is largely one of degree: as experimental confirmation accumulates we take a hypothesis more and more seriously, and as we map out its place in an overall theoretical scheme we become increasingly satisfied. But absolute and indubitable finality is not often available.

The reason Descartes did not see this may be twofold. First, he thinks that all reasoning can proceed deductively as in mathematics from initial axioms. But not all reasoning can be poured into a strictly deductive mold: attempts to take legal reasoning, historical methods, and moral reasoning that way, to name but three examples, have not been successful. Some deductive moves may be employed, but good judgment in those areas is far more complex and far more dependent on interpretive frameworks which construe evidence in particular ways. Second, Descartes takes his axioms to be self-evident and universal truths, as in the geometry of his day. But the doctrine of self-evident axioms is highly debatable. Axioms may just be useful postulates: Euclidean and non-Euclidean geometries employ different initial axioms, yet each has applications in the space-time world. And supposedly self-evident truths about man or morals, it is sometimes argued, only appear self-evident because of our historical and cultural conditioning.

We shall discuss further in chapter six this desire for indubitable first truths and deductive proofs, but enough has been said already to show that Descartes' hope is by no means assured fulfilment. At times our judgments have to be provisional, like progress reports, the best we can do with the resources at our disposal at that stage in our thinking. So in chapter seven we shall try to formulate the conditions under which less-than-conclusive judgments may be regarded as adequately justified beliefs.

## 4. Science and religion

One example of the provisional nature of our judgments concerns the tension between science and religion. This is not unique to Christianity but comes up in ancient Greece, in the history of Moslem thought, and elsewhere.

Notice first the role of "epistemological subjectivity." The attitude a man adopts to science and to religion will frequently determine how he handles particular issues. If he regards science with suspicion, he will be defensive about religious experience and doctrine. If he regards religion as childish, he will ignore its teachings. If he regards each as making legitimate contributions to an understanding of man and his world, he will take seriously and try somehow to interrelate what each has to say. But in any case one comes to particulars not with detached "epistemological objectivity" but with preconceptions about how in principle the two areas relate. One may modify or abandon this preconception under the pressure of subsequent evidence, but some prior attitude is humanly unavoidable. The kind of objectivity which starts with nothing but axiomatic truths or hard empirical data is non-existent. In view either of man's apparent need to see things as an interrelated whole or of supposed conflicts between religion and science, it is impossible to suspend judgment about the relation of scientific inquiry to religious belief. Our judgments are therefore provisional.

Consider next how errors of judgment arise and might be

avoided in this area. We are told that a particular scientific finding contradicts Christianity: for instance, the discovery that a
primitive living organism can be synthesized under laboratory
conditions might be supposed to contradict the doctrine of creation; or the construction of androids, robots programmed to simu-
late intelligent activities like playing chess or computing income
tax, might be supposed to deny the uniqueness ascribed in Scripture to man. How, then, can we reconcile science and religion?
*First,* we must be sure of our facts. On the one hand, exactly
what functions can man-made organisms or artificial intelligence
perform? It would not at present be honest to claim that they can
perform *all* human functions. On the other hand, exactly what
does the Bible teach about the nature of life and of man? That
God made every living thing does not imply that life is an entity
or force separate from the constituents of matter and that it is
neither explicable in biochemical terms nor subject to artificial
duplication. The artificial duplication of life in a laboratory
would simply mean that men have reproduced chemical composi-
tions God developed first. It would be equally erroneous to suppose that the Bible regards intelligence as man's entire uniqueness. Basic to the Biblical view of man, rather, is the account of
responsible agents whose historical acts are to be guided and
judged by the law of God, a law whose precepts and values they
must consciously make their own. There is thus an inwardness to
man as agent that cannot be described fully in terms of either his
logical processes or his overt behavior. Man is far more than what
he does. Nor should we jump from the Biblical term "soul" to
the kind of body-soul dualism which Plato and Descartes contributed to the intellectual tradition of the West. The Biblical concept
of soul is not identical with Descartes' "soul-substance" that
merely interacts causally with the body; nor is it the same as
Plato's view that the soul is an eternal form that rules the body by
reason. Nor yet can the Biblical concept of soul be surrendered to
some contemporary kind of materialism. Christianity is not
necessarily tied to Descartes' interactionism, nor to any other one
version of the mind-body relation, nor even to that way of posing
the problem. Biblically, "soul" simply denotes a living being;
the Bible speaks far more to the unity of personality than to
questions about man's constituent parts.

To relate science to Scripture at the level of particulars, therefore, requires first that we be sure of what both the scientific and

the Biblical facts are, rather than uncritically jumping to current conclusions on either side. It requires, *second,* that we interpret the facts aright: that we isolate them for consideration, analyze them, relate them to other facts, ascribe causes, and so on. Here our various interpretive frameworks become most evident: the Marxist and the Christian, for example, bring to social studies vastly different ideas about the causes that are at work, and their differing value-schemes lead them to different value judgments about events. Different interpretive schemes must themselves be examined and evaluated, and provisional judgments must be made on them. *Third,* we need to correlate the two sets of interpreted information—the scientific and the religious. They may at first seem to conflict if we have misinterpreted our facts or if we misconstrue the nature of scientific explanation, the nature of theological explanation, or their interrelations. We must understand how the two relate in principle before we can deal adequately with particulars.[1]

The complexity of the thing is, therefore, such that we often have to choose between alternative views and could well go wrong at a dozen places. Yet the value of understanding is such that we need to make provisional judgments and risk mistakes. We must therefore be self-critical and well informed; we must hedge what we say with a degree of tentativeness appropriate to the evidence in the case, and we must recognize that alternative possibilities exist. Our basic beliefs and our interpretive schemes matter most. If we are wrong in some particulars it is not likely to be fatal as long as "back-up systems" are possible. We must learn to live with fallibility just as we do with natural evil.

## 5. Philosophical errors

Philosophical issues, clearly, crop up in every area of the arts and sciences, so that here too provisional judgments are unavoidable. Nobody can even be introduced to philosophy without discover-

---

1. Hence the importance of the philosophy of science and the philosophy of religion. For an introductory discussion of these problems see Ian Barbour, *Issues in Science and Religion* (Prentice-Hall, 1966), and A.F. Holmes, *Faith Seeks Understanding* (Eerdmans, 1971), chapter one. Nicholas Wolterstorff discusses the bearing of religious and other "control beliefs" on theory formation generally in *Reason Within the Bounds of Religion* (Eerdmans, 1976).

ing its bewildering array of mutually incompatible positions. Some must be in error in at least some regards; perhaps all are in error, and the way philosophers go about things is mistaken, so that we should be sceptical about the whole philosophical enterprise. Does philosophy never settle anything? Then again some widely held philosophical positions conflict with Christianity, indeed with theism in general; one or the other is seemingly in error, and the novice either grows sceptical of Christianity or else becomes cynical about philosophy.

To appraise these situations we must understand the historical character of philosophical inquiry: we need to see it in the context of history as a whole, and in the light of the thesis that all truth is God's truth wherever it be found. Three views of history may be distinguished.

*First,* the sceptical view sees history in general as getting nowhere, and the history of philosophy as a prime example of its ineffectiveness. One philosophy succeeds another only to be refuted and replaced by others, just as in political history one world power succeeds another only to weaken and be surpassed by others. History makes no real progress and neither does philosophy. Descartes, for instance, is sceptical about past philosophers, their disagreements and their errors, and Francis Bacon criticizes them as "idols of the market place." Yet both of them are much more optimistic about the philosophy of the future, provided it practices the new methods they propose. Sceptics today are not always so optimistic about something new.

I have difficulty reconciling this sort of pessimism, whether about philosophy or about human history generally, with Christian belief. The Bible views history as the arena of God's creative and redemptive activity. For all their failures, Israelite and even pagan cultures bear witness to the creator and remain deeply involved in the creation mandate. History, moreover, has been penetrated by God's revelation in Christ so as to bear the still clearer imprint of his truth and grace. The history of mankind is vastly changed by the presence of Christianity, and so is the history of philosophy. For these reasons it is hard to suppose that either history in general or the history of philosophy in particular has no place in God's providence, and no positive contribution to make. It would take a pessimism that seems unchristian to surrender to scepticism.

*Second,* an overly optimistic view sees history evolving in one grand direction towards some utopian state and sees philosophy moving towards an overall synthesis that will incorporate the truth of lesser positions into a final and complete system of truth, the whole truth, and nothing but the truth. In one form this was the view of the nineteenth century philosopher Hegel, who applied his evolutionary philosophy of history to the history of philosophy, tracing its dialectical path to the emergence of the greatest and most inclusive system of all—which he himself developed.

Both the sceptical and the optimistic views leave much to be desired, for they both expect of philosophy a kind of inevitable progress that is perhaps more appropriate to science than to the humanities and to culture generally. The progress of scientific knowledge is largely cumulative, despite the occasional reshaping of scientific models that initiates scientific revolutions and despite misuses of scientific technology. Progress in the humanities is different: new methods are developed, new input from the sciences and from other aspects of history is assimilated, but we still work with the same basic questions and ideas. Literature and art have always given themselves to picturing creatively the human significance of things and their aesthetic, moral, emotional, and existential value. Greek sculpture and drama, therefore, have a lasting value for the contemporaneity of what they saw as well as for their antiquity and technique, and the Greek view of life continues to influence modern world-views in one way or another. So it is with philosophy. A. N. Whitehead said that the whole history of philosophy is a series of footnotes to Plato. While new methods and new arguments are developed and new input from the sciences and other aspects of history is assimilated, philosophy itself is concerned with questions that are foundational to life and thought in any age, and which need constant examination. Philosophical judgments are therefore provisional, subject always to correction and counter-argument, rather than cumulative. The inevitability of progress is by no means assured.

Consequently, a *third* view of history is required, less optimistic than the evolutionary view of Hegel yet less pessimistic than the scepticism with which Bacon and Descartes regarded the past. Such a *via media,* it seems to me, is consonant with a Biblical view of history and with the limits which human finiteness and sin impose on both life and thought. Yet it gladly admits God's goodness in human culture and learning.

To apply the third view of history to philosophy in a way that explains both its merits and its mistakes requires a closer look at what goes into the making of a philosophical position.[2] Several elements must be distinguished.

(1) Perennial *problems* provide the matrix within which philosophy operates. They concern human knowledge and belief (epistemology), the nature of reality (philosophy of nature, philosophy of mind, philosophical theology, etc.), and human values (ethics, aesthetics, etc.). These problem areas underlie all other aspects of life and thought in every period of history; they are basic to education, to politics, to art criticism, to religion. But some problems are more to the fore at one time than another, and this helps shape philosophical positions. The problem of permanence and change in the philosophy of nature, for instance, did much to shape the Greek theory of universals; the problem of knowledge shaped the Enlightenment view of man; and the problem of meaning shapes much contemporary thought.

(2) Historical *periods* can be distinguished, as in the history of ideas generally, by their characteristic values and beliefs. Accordingly we distinguish ancient from medieval and modern periods and subdivide the modern period into Renaissance, Enlightenment, and Romanticism, each characterized in ways that find expression in the social institutions, the art, and the philosophy of the period. These historical differences further differentiate positions.

(3) Differing *scientific models* for understanding nature and man have been developed. First came the Greek model of eternal forms that structure the material world and give life and intelligibility to nature, then the mechanistic model of fixed forces or laws of motion imposed on material particles, then a more dynamic model stemming from the concept of evolution, relativity physics, and electromagnetic field theory. The first was systematically stated by Aristotle and controlled most of Western science, philosophy, theology, politics, and art until the Renaissance. The second as developed by Newton dominated Western culture until the nineteenth century and is still in evidence today.

---

2. I am more concerned here with overall philosophical positions, sometimes known as ''systematic,'' than with the activity of doing philosophy or with relatively isolated questions of more professional interest. Similar observations might be made in those regards, but the overall positions are more important both historically and in regard to world-views and the unity of truth.

The third finds expression in evolutionary ideas generally and in romanticism and humanism, not only in philosophy but also in theology, education, literature, and the arts.[3] The first two models are far from extinct, so that current disagreements between philosophical positions often stem from the use of conflicting scientific models. Contrast, for example, Thomism with behaviorism and with the pragmatism of Dewey or Joseph Fletcher. Thomism employs the Aristotelian model, behaviorism clings closer to a modified mechanistic model, whereas Dewey and Fletcher employ the evolutionary.

(4) A variety of *methods* have developed, some of them (but not all) derived from the scientific model in use. Plato's dialectic was geared to understanding eternal ideas or forms that stand in another world than that of physical experience. The scholastic method of starting with first principles reflects Aristotle's organization of nature into genera and species, each defined in terms of its own formal cause. Descartes' intuitive and deductive procedures were drawn from the mathematical methods he found so successful in mechanistic science. Some of the analytic methods employed in English-speaking philosophy today arose in the reaction of metaphysical pluralists against the monism of English idealists early in this century. The phenomenological methods of European philosophy stem from the influence of nineteenth century idealism. Methodological differences, themselves highly complex, account for a great amount of philosophical disagreement.

(5) In addition to differences in problems, periods, models, and methods we find that philosophical positions differ in their underlying *perspective* or *world-view*. Writers like Dooyeweerd, Cornelius Van Til, and Francis Schaeffer tend to make this the all-consuming difference and so underestimate the other differentiating factors. Undoubtedly this factor holds more religious interest than the others and undoubtedly it is related to the others. But it does not by itself explain all the disagreements, for Christian philosophers as well as others hold a variety of positions. On the other hand, some writers tend to ignore "perspectival" influences as if it were possible to ignore "epistemological subjectiv-

---

3. On those models and their cultural effect, see A.N. Whitehead, *Science and the Modern World* (Macmillan, 1925), and F.W. Matson, *The Broken Image* (Anchor Books, 1966).

ity'' generally. But the world-view is after all part, perhaps the most important part, of what the human subject brings to his quest for truth.

At least three major perspectives run through the history of thought: naturalistic, idealistic, and theistic. The first systematically explains everything in terms of physical elements or events, and produces materialistic and naturalistic philosophies that vary with the problems they stress (Marxism for instance focusses on social and economic philosophy, while Hobbes starts with psychology), with their historical period and its distinctive emphases (Hobbes stresses the rule of reason's laws which Marcuse criticizes), with scientific models (Hobbes' mechanism vs. Dewey's evolutionary models), and with philosophical method (Hobbes' deductive procedure vs. the analysis of contemporary materialists). Yet all of these men share a common naturalistic world-view.

Within philosophical idealism Plato, Berkeley, and Hegel are far apart in the problems they emphasize, in their historical setting and in their models and methods, yet they share a common perspective that explains everything in terms of immaterial realities.

Similarly, theists make various attempts to explain nature's and man's dependence on a transcendent and personal creator-God. Jewish, Moslem, and Christian philosophers differ, and so do Christians like Augustine, Descartes, William Temple, and Herman Dooyeweerd; yet they share a basic theistic perspective. Theism like other perspectival traditions is pluralistic, and no one factor can suffice in accounting for its inner philosophical disagreements. Religious differences contribute because they shape both the personal and the theoretical meaning of the theistic perspective, so that Moslems may differ philosophically from Christians, Catholics from Protestants, and Anabaptists from Reformed thinkers. But not all philosophical differences can be reduced to theological differences; for the problems emphasized, the historical periods in which a position is rooted, the models and methods employed all make a difference.

Naturalism, idealism, and theism are all perspectival and pluralistic traditions. They are also holistic in that the perspective provides an integrative overview, a skeletal outline of how to systematize things as a whole. And they are exploratory in that the perspective is a starting point which does not itself resolve all the problems philosophy faces. But it provides a point of view from which to explore philosophical matters.[4]

Now this account of what makes a philosophic position what it is points up the maze of ways in which disagreement and error can arise. It makes it plain that philosophical error is not all due to sin and unbelief or to the misuse of human free will. Some error is due, like natural evil, to human finiteness, to the highly complicated nature of things, and to the impracticability of always suspending judgment. The possibility of error is so closely interwoven into the process of life and thought that it cannot be avoided. We must therefore learn to accept our fallibility and not be paralyzed by feelings of guilt or inadequacy. We must work towards alleviating the consequences of error just as we would work at alleviating the painful consequences of natural evil. We should not expect philosophical unanimity, even among Christian thinkers, but should gladly open ourselves to criticism and correction.

## 6. Why does God allow it?

That error is an inevitable ingredient of human thought suggests to the Christian that in the final analysis it has purpose. Descartes preferred to leave God's purposes to the theologians, but really no Christian can altogether avoid speculating as to why God makes things the way they are. We know that ultimately both natural evil and moral evil will be overcome with good, just as death will be swallowed up in victory, but what do natural evil and natural error contribute here and now to the purposes of God?

First, error can teach us. A child learns to do arithmetic by practice and makes mistakes in the process; he learns mathematical concepts and he develops a precise and disciplined mind by his mistakes, perhaps more than he would by giving right answers to easy questions. A university student learns to argue philosophically by preparing a paper that may contain logical mistakes, historical errors, and conceptual confusions. But to write that paper and have it carefully criticized is essential to the learning process. Even a "bad error" can eventually serve the good. Human finiteness implies capacity for growth, and in-

---

4. This perspectival nature of philosophy is expounded in more detail in this author's *Christian Philosophy in the Twentieth Century* (Craig Press, 1969).

tellectual growth implies exposing our fallibility, sharpening our logical tools, honing our concepts into shape. It is painful but good.

Second, a Christian in philosophy will find himself wrestling with the same problems as others by means of similar models and methods. He accordingly has a basis for dialog with and for benefitting from the work of non-Christians. He need not practice intellectual isolationism, and dare not if he is to examine his own ideas and those of others with an honesty that leaves no skeletons in the closet and sweeps no dust under the rug. The Christian student should take to heart the Biblical reminder that "God has not given us a spirit of fear," and shun any obscurantist avoidance of critical problems. All truth is God's truth, wherever and however it be found.

Third, the fact that we learn from others with different perspectives from our own suggests that neither we nor they are either completely right or completely wrong. Rather a position may be true to some extent and in some regards and false in others. Sometimes a student will ask of a given assertion, "Is that right or not?" To which I answer "Yes," and go on to explain what may be right about it and what may be wrong. Blanket judgments must give way to careful and critical discernment.

Fourth, our account of what shapes philosophical positions provides a guide to the critical evaluation of their views and arguments. In some cases disagreement may be apparent rather than fundamental, more like calling "check!" than "check mate!" or even settling for a "stale mate." Disagreement might be resolved by making limited changes, by qualifying what is said, or by relating opposing positions to some larger and more embracing view. The latter occurs in philosophy of science when the principle of complementarity is invoked to preserve both the corpuscular and the wavular nature of light. But in other cases reconciliation is impossible and criticisms must be pressed, and then it is valuable to scrutinize the elements that allow for disagreement.

One might argue that a certain man, John, will modify his view of man if he considers the problem of human responsibility rather than just the behavioral matters on which he now concentrates. This criticism attacks the limited nature of his original *problem*.

Alternatively one might argue that John's view of man, while firmly rooted in the work of important eighteenth century thinkers, has not sufficiently taken into account nineteenth and twentieth century insights into human personality. This criticism singles out the *historical* milieu for examination.

Or one might argue that John is working with a mechanistic *model* when he speaks of behavioral conditioning.

Or one might criticize John's *method*. A purely empirical approach limits what we can say about man.

Finally, different *perspectives* may be the focus of criticism. It is as important to recognize the consequences of adopting materialistic presuppositions, for example, as it is to understand what theism suggests about truth and error, good and evil, freedom and determinism, and so on. A perspective may be criticized because its basic presuppositions are inadequately supported, or because its larger implications are unacceptable. Thus, C. S. Lewis criticized naturalism for the difficulty it has in justifying both rational judgments and moral judgments.[5] The Christian will be most concerned to detect errors that arise either from adopting non-Christian perspectives or from not consistently following a Christian perspective, and he will be more tolerant of errors that are due to other elements in philosophizing. By the same token, the person who is satisfied that Christianity (or some other perspective for that matter) is true, and who understands the essential ingredients of his faith, is not likely to be as philosophically confused on problems where the implications of his perspective are plain.

Similar influences may be identified in other fields than philosophy. Our *de*partments of learning are not airtight *com*partments: they share a common history and their different subject matters are interrelated. The history of literature and the arts, for example, also shows the effect of focussing on various *problems,* often of a technical sort. We can distinguish different historical *periods,* and characterize Enlightenment or Renaissance art accordingly. We can trace the influence of changing scientific *models,* not only in the ideas they express but also in the way they depict things. *Methods* and techniques change too; and the artist's *world-view* shows up in various ways, both in his choice of subject and in his handling of it.

We need to understand these influences if we are to evaluate a work of art or a literary piece, just as we need to in evaluating a

---

5. See his *Miracles* (Geoffrey Bles, 1947), chapters two through five.

philosophical position.[6] Artists too err. They may fail to handle their problem effectively; their techniques may be inadequate to the task; they may misinterpret what they portray, or make mistaken value judgments; like T. S. Eliot or François Mauriac they may well express an essentially Christian world-view, or like Sartre and Camus they may deliberately express a totally different perspective.

Nobody can honestly avoid asking whether an artist tells us the truth or not. Nor can the Christian back away, either from difficult and touchy subjects or from the critical work that goes with thinking for oneself. On matters of cardinal importance to the Christian faith, Scripture makes the contours of truth clear; this in turn provides perspective in related areas. On many other matters we can simply agree to disagree, even when we cannot withhold judgment. On some there is no way to make sound judgments without painstaking thought.

Thus we are confronted with a new set of problems: the relation of revelation to reason, the trustworthiness of human reasoning, and the problem of justifying the judgments we make. These are our topics in the next three chapters.

---

6. A book like H.R. Rookmaaker's *Modern Art and the Death of a Culture* tends to evaluate art works in terms of the artist's world-view, to the neglect of other formative factors. By doing so, it is often over-critical, seeing religious significance where historical and aesthetic considerations may have weighed more heavily.

# FIVE

# No Royal Road

In previous chapters we attempted to remove two stumbling blocks in the way of a Christian's pursuit of truth: first, the popular dichotomy of sacred and secular learning that values the former but regards the latter as unimportant and, second, the simplistic expectation of overcoming human fallibility and altogether avoiding error. We can neither compartmentalize truth nor ignore "secular learning" nor dodge hard questions nor avoid making mistakes. The only way to a correct understanding of anything is to work ever more carefully at the intellectual task.

At this juncture some Christians may propose that the believer travels a royal road to learning, a shorter and surer way to truth than the hazardous intellectual path. We know by faith, they say. God has so revealed truth that we no longer need to travel the long way around, even if that road were open. Or we learn all we need to know from life itself and firsthand from our experience of God. These royal roads we shall now explore far enough to see that by themselves they do not lead us to a sufficiently complete and careful understanding of things secular and sacred for all our purposes. It is not that faith fails in its task, that God's revelation is false, or that firsthand experience has no value. Rather as we examine faith, revelation, and experience, we shall discover that their purposes do not altogether coincide with the purposes of human learning. They are necessary but insufficient. They overlap with our quest for truth and they contribute indispensably to it, but that is all. There is no royal road to learning.

## 1. Faith and truth

What is faith? We are thinking of religious faith and of the Christian's faith in particular, for while the term has wider uses (e.g. "faith in human nature," "faith in the government," "keeping faith with one's friends"), these are not as directly pertinent to our inquiry. Moreover, in speaking of religious faith we are not thinking primarily of its doctrinal content, but of the act of believing. What is it to "have faith in God"? Do we know truth by faith?

First, faith is man's response to God's self-revelation. It is a human act elicited by God's action. In the Bible, John's Gospel offers a series of pictures of faith, of which three will suffice. First, faith is like receiving a person (John 1:10–12) rather than ignoring or rejecting him. We readily grasp the analogy today because of the emphasis on accepting people rather than "putting them down." To receive a person is to listen to him, to make him part of your life, to be open, responsive, and appreciative. In the New Testament faith is more than these phrases now convey: to receive Christ is to open oneself to *all* he wants to do in our lives, and so to be made into children of God (John 1:12).

Again, John depicts faith as a desperate cry for help. His illustration is the Old Testament story of the Israelites in the wilderness who, when bitten by poisonous snakes, were saved by obediently turning to a bronze snake God told Moses to make for that purpose (John 3:14–15). John pictures faith in Christ similarly as a man's only hope. Faith is turning out of desperation to receive God's grace.

Again, after the feeding of the 5000 Jesus pictures faith as eating and drinking, and he illustrates it by reference to the manna and the water provided for the Israelites during their wilderness journey (John 6:25–35). Faith is the act of taking and of making my own what God provides. Faith assimilates his grace into my life.

Faith, then, is man's response to God, the opening of our lives to him. Faith is more than assent to true propositions (credal assent). To some extent that is involved, for he who comes to God "must believe that he exists and that he rewards those who seek him" (Heb. 11:6). But credal assent is not enough. James points out that in that sense of faith the devil believes—and trembles. Religious faith includes trust, openness, consent, and commitment, as well as assent. It is the response of the whole person to the revelation of God's grace that transforms his life. Faith, then, is not itself a source of new information or a mysterious kind of learning process, but openness to what is already revealed; it interiorizes what we already know. It enriches and enlivens knowledge; it is likely, therefore, to produce both conviction about and obedience to what is otherwise a detached sort of knowledge. But faith itself is not knowledge.

Theologians express this in a variety of ways. Charles Hodge, the nineteenth century Presbyterian divine, points out that just as the primary idea of truth is trustworthiness, so the primary idea of faith is a voluntary trust in the trustworthy.[1] The Baptist theologian A.H. Strong captures the personal character of faith by means of a three-faculty psychology: faith contains both an intellectual element and emotional and volitional ingredients.[2] The Reformed systematician Louis Berkhof follows a similar procedure.[3]

Søren Kierkegaard speaks of faith as passion and subjectivity. As we noted previously, "passion" means not simply emotion but rather a depth of involvement which detached intellectual processes lack. Kierkegaard criticizes the objective reason and scholarly detachment of the Enlightenment, pointing out that the best of their conclusions are qualitatively and not just quantitatively different from that decisive faith with which a man devotes his whole life to God. Such a faith is his "passion." Likewise, Kierkegaard regards subjectivity not as a private and purely relative opinion, but as the total involvement of a fully personal subject in his beliefs and actions.[4]

Paul Tillich similarly speaks of faith as the ultimate concern of the total personality.[5] It is a "centered" act at the very heart of one's life that brings all else into a unifying focus: it unites the subconscious with the conscious, the rational with the emotional and volitional, subjectivity with objectivity.

The relation between faith and reason should be understood accordingly as the relation of the whole person, with his most basic and inclusive commitment, to his intellectual activities. It is a whole-to-part relation, rather than part-to-part. Reason properly operates under the motivation of faith, with the purposefulness of faith, with the integrity and humility and teachableness of faith, and its path is illuminated by knowing what it is the person so heartily believes.

---

1. *Systematic Theology* (Eerdmans, 1952), vol. III, p. 42.
2. *Systematic Theology* (Judson Press, 1907), pp. 836–848.
3. *Systematic Theology* (Eerdmans, 1949), pp. 503–506.
4. See *Concluding Unscientific Postscript* (Princeton University Press, 1944).
5. *The Dynamics of Faith* (Harper Torchbooks, 1957), chapters one and two.

"By faith we understand that the world was created . . ." (Heb. 11:3) does not mean that faith is itself either a source of knowledge or a substitute for knowing, but that the whole person's faith in God includes an understanding that God is the creator and that this affords the starting point for further thought. Faith gives perspective to reason, but it has no royal road to learning that can bypass difficult questions and hard thinking. The Christian believer knows God to be the ultimate source of all truth. In principle, all truth is God's truth. But the working out of this principle in regard to all the arts and sciences as well as theology is a job that reason itself must do.

This conclusion bears on two previous observations. First, faith is analogous to "epistemological subjectivity" (chapter three) in that it is the dominant and unifying feature in what the believer is and does as a person, in his subjecthood. What he is as a believer affects how and what he thinks. His subjectivity is not itself a source or way of knowledge but the way in which as a human subject he relates to the truth he knows, treating it with the utmost seriousness and making it his own. He is open to the truth and eager to learn. He is spiritually receptive. As the apostle said, "spiritual things are spiritually discerned." Dooyeweerd speaks of a ground-*motive* because a man's religious faith both informs and motivates his further inquiry.

Second, faith is analogous to the perspective of a world-view (chapter four) in that it affords a starting point from which to see things whole. Faith is not just a set of doctrines added to what we know by reason alone, but rather a stance towards God which affords a vantage point from which to explore things secular and sacred in relationship to the creator. Faith is not closed-minded but exploratory; it does not compartmentalize life but unifies it; and it allows a plurality of possible positions because it is not itself the source of knowledge.

## 2. Revelation and truth

Granted that faith is man's response to God and not itself a source of knowledge or way of knowing, what about the divine revelation to which faith responds? Has God not revealed the truth? Is the Bible not a royal road to learning?

Here we run into sensitive and complex questions. What do we mean by revelation? Is it a source of information regarding the truth or does it only provide an intense experience of God which then engenders thought? The former alternative, that revelation informs us of the truth, is the historical view held by orthodox Christians and frequently labelled "propositional revelation," whereas the latter is more characteristic of liberal and existential theology.

We need to be careful in defining "propositional." In the first place, revelation is *not only* informative *but also* personal and redemptive: that is to say, God discloses *himself* to men and does so in order to elicit their faith in his saving grace. The propositional content of revelation is not information for information's sake, but has a personal and redemptive intent. In the second place, "propositional" creates misleading expectations. The layman tends to think of God-given statements of a quasi-scientific sort, whereas in fact revelation is primarily about historical events and situations whose moral, theological, and redemptive significance is interpreted by the Biblical writers. The term "propositional" is useful if we understand that it means Biblical revelation has cognitive content, that it informs us about revelatory events and their meaning, and that it is true both in the sense of trustworthiness and in the sense of making true judgments. Some philosophical traditions regard a proposition as an extra-linguistic and extra-mental state of affairs that is objectively what it is. In those terms propositional revelation would be about the "metaphysical objectivity" of God and his dealings with men.

During the Enlightenment a more limited conception of propositional revelation was current. John Locke, for instance, defined revelation as the communication of true propositions, some of which go beyond what can be discovered by reason alone. He regarded knowledge as the purely objective joining and separating of clear and distinct ideas: our reasoning starts with simple intuitive or else empirical ideas, joins them into complex ideas, and then draws inferences. Thus, my knowledge of other persons depends on arguments from the analogy between what I observe of my own bodily behavior and what I observe of theirs, and my knowledge of God's existence is inferred from the intuitive ideas of my own existence. Truth consists in the agreement of my ideas and judgments with their external objects, and knowledge is at best a mental copy of the things to which it corresponds.

For Locke, revelation fits this pattern.[6] It saves us making difficult and sometimes impossible inferences concerning God and his works by presenting us with true propositions over and above what we know by natural means. Its truth consists simply in the correspondence of its propositions with the objective facts it describes. Our knowledge of God is accordingly a knowledge of true propositions about God, just as our knowledge of other persons consists of true propositions about them.

The problem with this is that it confines knowledge to an objective awareness of true propositions without a more whole-person experience, so that it accepts propositional truth independently of personal fidelity.

It was against these limitations that nineteenth and twentieth century theologians reacted. Friedrich Schleiermacher, the theologian of the German romanticist movement, described true religion instead as the experience of absolute dependence on the All-Encompassing Being that pervades and embraces all of nature and all men. This experiential view of revelation became the basis of liberal theology, in that it left men to distill doctrine from religious experience rather than learning it from what the Bible teaches. Whereas the Enlightenment tended to make revelation entirely propositional and not at all a direct experience of God, Schleiermacher and liberal theology make it entirely experiential and not at all propositional.

In our day existential theology has taken liberalism's place, with the claim that a royal road to truth exists, a way of encountering the divine ground of our being. Paul Tillich revises the account of religious experience from a benign feeling of dependence to an anxiety-laden disclosure of the depths of human despair, in which our ultimate concern demands a ground of being. God then becomes the source of our courage to be, but few informative propositions about God are possible. To say, for example, that God is personal means only that he grounds our personal existence by giving us the courage to be authentically ourselves, not that he himself is a person in whose image we are created. Tillich's theology thus projects onto God what man's

---

6. For an account of how theories of revelation reflect more general theories of knowledge, see H.D. Macdonald, *Ideas of Revelation* (Macmillan, 1959) and *Theories of Revelation* (Humanities Press, 1963).

existential predicament requires that he be. Doctrine is a purely
human distillation from religious experience, and since revelation
is purely existential and not at all propositional it draws attention
to the human condition and to the dynamics of faith and courage
rather than informing us about God. Its truth consists in its power
of existential disclosure rather than in objective and cognitive
content. Consequently it affords no royal road to propositional
truth about God, and theological relativism results.

Even in more conservative existential theologies than Tillich's,
a similar separation of the personal and the propositional persists.
Emil Brunner sees revelation as personal confrontation, an "I-
Thou" experience of God conceived on the model of Martin
Buber's distinction between interpersonal experience with others
as human subjects (I-Thou) and the more detached relationships
(I-It) in which we treat things and propositions and even people as
objects. When I talk about a person or my relationship to him, I
make him an object instead of a subject; I depersonalize him and
reduce the I-Thou experience to the I-It level. For Brunner, revelation is a direct personal encounter with God (I-Thou). Propositions about God (I-It) reduce God to an object of thought and
thereby falsify the truth of the encounter. The Bible is *about* (I-It)
God's personal revelation (I-Thou), and not itself a divine revelation to men. Accordingly it remains a fallible human witness to
God's revelation and can provide no royal road to learning, however insightful its witness may be.

These historical examples should help us focus the relation of
revelation to truth. The Enlightenment stressed propositional revelation, but in such a way as to reduce revelation to objectively
true propositions apart from personal encounter, because it regarded knowledge and truth alike as wholly propositional and not
at all personal or subjective. Nineteenth and twentieth century
theologians deny propositional revelation and stress religious and
existential experience, because they value direct experience and
personal truth over and above objective knowledge and propositional truth. The problem is that we have separated the personal
from the propositional, and subjectivity from objectivity.

From the beginning of this book we have been trying to see
how epistemological subjectivity may be united with metaphysical objectivity, and how personal truth relates to true propositions. Science involves degrees of subjectivity, and philosophy
is perspectival. The Biblical conception of truth covers the sub-

jective or personal pole as well as the objective or propositional, and the Biblical conception of knowledge follows the same pattern. We see now that the Biblical conception of revelation likewise embraces both subjective and objective poles: revelation is propositional and informative, but it is also personal, redemptive, and experiential. In Scripture God is in direct touch with men, and they seek personal communion with him. He acts in their lives and they respond. Their language about God is neither depersonalized "I-It" talk nor only the language of personal address ("I-Thou"), but also stories about his deeds and talk of love and trust ("I-He"). "The Lord is my shepherd: I shall not want." Subject-object dichotomies break down in the face of this. The two alternatives become rather the poles of a continuum within which relationships may be more or less direct and personal and at the same time cognitive, so that they reveal a person's subjecthood with varying degrees both of intimacy and objectivity. To change the image, it is not either-or but both-and, a "both" that is possible because of a whole-and-part relation in which the personal is the whole and the objective a part.

In sum, revelation is not *either* personal *or* propositional, but both. A person reveals himself, as does God, by what he does and says, and by what others do and say in response. Propositional revelation thereby informs us about the personal nature of God. The language of the Bible is after all not that of an eighteenth century scientific treatise, but that of the humanities—history, biography, poetry, philosophy of life, correspondence, social criticism, and so forth. In its immense variety it has a hundred ways of informing us of the character of both God and men and of interpreting the acts of God to men.

Granted that revelation is thus a source of both personal and propositional knowledge and not an inscrutable experience, does it provide that royal road to learning about which we have been asking?

In the first place, revelation is not a source of information about everything. It is the Christian's "final and sufficient rule for faith and practice," but it is not exhaustive, not even on matters of doctrine and morality, let alone on other subjects. The Bible is not a textbook for science, nor even a sufficient source for ancient Near Eastern history or for a knowledge of the Hebrew and Greek languages. We need and have other sources of information on such matters. The Bible is not a royal road to learning everything.

In the second place, while it is our normative source of information on matters of faith and practice, like any informational source it must be studied and interpreted. It does not bypass either reason or objective inquiry. Reading requires thought, and so does reading the Bible. Biblical exegesis requires hard thinking about ancient languages, grammar and syntax, and the historical and literary contexts. Theology is an intellectual activity that submits itself to objective facts and propositions: it draws together scattered Biblical teaching on a particular topic, relates that topic to other topics, and understands it in relation to the input we have from other sources of knowledge. The Biblical doctrine of sin, for example, is studied as a whole and in relation to the doctrine of man and of divine grace, and with regard to the insights of psychology and sociology. Apologetics takes us still further in showing good reasons for what we believe. And all of these rational activities have still not taken us beyond Biblical and theological studies into the thinking a Christian must do in the arts and sciences. If a royal road is one which bypasses human reason, then no royal road to learning lies in the propositional revelation of Scripture.

In the third place, when Christians speak of the infallible truth of Scripture they do not claim infallibility for any of their own rational activities in the use of Scripture. Textual criticism is a fallible science; we can misread the text and misunderstand it even when we read it aright; our knowledge of the Biblical languages may be at fault, our hermeneutic misguided, or our generalizations about a Biblical teaching incomplete; theologians err and apologists may spend their energies defending a theologian's mistakes. The problem of error haunts us still.

This is the point behind the Reformers' insistence that Scripture alone (*sola Scriptura*) is the infallible rule of faith and practice, and behind the insistence that infallibility applies only to the original manuscripts of the Biblical writers. Does this mean that the texts we now have and our understanding of them are so riddled with errors as to be untrustworthy? The usual response, I think, is sound: that careful science in textual criticism assures us of all but an inconsequential fraction of the original Biblical text, that careful linguistic science assures us of reliable translations, and that careful exegesis and theology leave no doubt about the essentials of Biblical doctrine and morality. In all essentials of faith and practice, we have more than sufficient assurance of the content of the original manuscripts and can be confident in the conclusions we draw from them.

In the fourth place, our discussion of truth as personal trustworthiness makes a further response possible. When God spoke with personal fidelity to the prophets and apostles who produced the Biblical writings, he did so with the intent of speaking through them to us. His fidelity can therefore also be expected in the transmission and interpretation of those writings. This does not mean that the translator, the exegete, or the theologian become miraculously infallible (*sola Scriptura* in the Reformers' rule), but that Scripture lies open to honest and careful study, and the Spirit of God thereby leads open-minded men to the truth it teaches. Theologians appropriately maintain that the trustworthiness of what we now believe is due not only to careful textual and theological science, but also to the continued fidelity of the divine author of Scripture. The Spirit of God is the Spirit of truth.

It follows that man's rational work with Scripture or anything else cannot be conducted independently of God. The autonomy of human reason is a fiction. In God's creation nothing is altogether autonomous, and God can be relied on to secure the effective communication to men of his special revelation. If reason is not autonomous but depends on God, then God may well secure his ends through our intellectual activities, through what we are as human subjects and what he has made us to be. At this level also, subjectivity and objectivity alike are involved.

Finally, propositional revelation is by its very nature addressed to men as rational beings, capable of textual study, exegesis, and all the theological sciences. Nobody who believes in an informative revelation can consistently depreciate man's rational powers. On the contrary, such a revelation, entrusted as it is to fallible but rational men, bears eloquent testimony to the confidence God has both in the rational powers he gave to men and in man's ability to make reasoned judgments at least regarding the Scriptures.

## 3. Experience and truth

Before considering in more detail the nature and limits of human reasoning, we must examine one further possibility of a royal road to learning. Granted that faith affords no such avenue because it embraces reason, and granted that revelation does not exclude reason because it is addressed to rational men, what about ordinary human experience? Perhaps experience is a great enough teacher by itself for us to get along without the risks and the rigor of intellectual pursuits. If we have firsthand experience of God, what more do we want? In morality too we learn with experience, and likewise in social relationships and many arts and crafts. After all, isn't *experience* what it is all about?

To this question I have to reply with an unequivocal "No!" Experience is of course valuable and enriching, but it is *not* what life or religion is ultimately about. Experiences can be induced by hypnosis and fantasy, and religious-like experiences by hallucinatory drugs; moral experience often teaches us too little and too late. Not experience but *truth* is what it is all about. The truth about God and our relationship to him is far more important than the feeling-tones of religious experience, and the truth about moral right and moral wrong is more basic than "feeling right about it" or "learning the hard way." The truth does not change; experience does. Truth is universal and normative; experience is not. Truth is not a cold abstraction to be feared but has personal dimensions to allure and satisfy us. The truth is what really matters in the final count, for it will ultimately judge what we do and experience. Therefore, we must conform experience to the truth rather than truth to fluctuating experience. We must know the truth in order to be free.

But why can experience alone not lead us to truth? First, our experience is always incomplete and its horizon is limited in scope. Experience introduces only the things we experience whereas the truth we seek is universal and includes things we have not yet experienced and perhaps cannot. The future lies beyond our experience, yet it and other unexperienced aspects of existence allure us or otherwise affect us all the time.

Second, experience is selective. We do not notice everything within the scope of our perceptual horizon, but we cull from it according to our interests, attention, and purpose. An artist sees something in everyday objects that others of us never notice, and a lover catches fleeting facial expressions that a more casual observer overlooks.

Third, experience is relative. What we observe depends on where we stand in relation to an object: a coin may appear round, elliptical, or a straight line, depending on the angle of vision. What we observe also depends on the intervening medium: a clear or a foggy day, glasses on or off, and so forth. It depends on the observer's physical and psychological condition: alert or fatigued, shortsighted or emotionally distracted. Religious experience likewise is relative: the experience of awe in worship is hard to sustain amid physical fatigue or emotional distraction, yet it may be aided by the symbolism of church architecture, by hearing organ music, or by recalling the words of a prayer or a psalm; and what evokes religious experience for one generation or one culture may turn others off instead.

Fourth, experience is subject to interpretation. We often interpret what we experience so unconsciously that by the time we become aware of something we have already made judgments about it. In fact, it is questionable whether "raw experiences" ever occur. Rather, experience seems to be partly interpretive; the "facts" of experience are more "interprefacts" than they are bare. Religious experience is such a case. The believer is quick to claim that he meets with God, that God told him something, or that he learned such and such from his experience with God. Biblical characters speak that way, too. Believers in all sorts of religions make similar claims, but the "truths" they learn are sometimes contradictory, and the Christian hesitates to allow the Moslem's claim to the sort of meeting with God that he believes is available only through Jesus Christ. So we are forced to think that truth is not drawn directly from experience, but that we bring to experience beliefs which are thereby illuminated and reinforced. As a result we suppose them to be taught by experience itself.

When we look at religious experience more closely we realize that the claim to have met God is actually interpretive, for one does not see God himself or hear an indisputably divine voice in which God unmistakably identifies himself. What we actually experience has been variously described as a feeling of awe, a sense of the numinous, a presence, and so forth. It is an awareness in which the object of awareness remains indistinct and undefined. The Christian interprets it as a meeting with God because he believes that God, by his Holy Spirit, meets those who humbly seek him repenting for sin and trusting in Christ's mercy. But the uninterpreted awareness, that feeling of awe, is apparently experienced in other religious contexts and under the influence of drugs in no religious setting at all. What counts, then, is not the experience but the truth about the experience and the God we encounter.

A number of years ago my wife accompanied me to a meeting sponsored by Christian students at a certain university. After my address, as we talked informally with some international students who had been invited, she spoke to one of them of her experience of peace and joy as a Christian. The student, a Moslem, applauded this and assured her that he too experienced peace and joy in the Islamic faith. The truth question remained untouched by experience alone, for the experience of peace and joy is not self-interpreting; it affords no royal road to truth. Yet in the final analysis it is the truth of Christianity that counts, not just enriching experience.

The same conclusion arises when one examines the testimony of medieval mystics. Mystic experience itself may yield no knowledge but be rather an ecstatic awareness of the ineffable. For some, the mystic path is an inner discipline and introspection in which they withdraw from all consciousness of the world, then move beyond conscious thought through a dark hole in the inner recesses of the soul to union with the divine. But this very account presupposes that God is to be found within the soul, that he lies beyond thought, and that the physical world leads us away from him rather than to him. These are neo-Platonic presuppositions that assume a very unchristian valuation of both body and mind. But in any case they indicate that mystic experience does not necessarily lead to truth; instead, it may assume as true what in fact is false.

To experiment today with the occult or with Eastern mysticism in order to find truth similarly begs the question and inverts the relation of experience to truth. What we provisionally judge to be true shapes what we do and what we experience. To experiment honestly with Eastern mysticism requires that one adopt, overtly or tacitly, its pantheistic presuppositions, but these need careful and critical assessment. The truth question simply cannot be left in abeyance while we see what kind of religious experience we like or can most readily achieve.

Experimental approaches to truth can mislead us, if they are not carefully scrutinized. Experiments tell whether a procedure will achieve its goals, but they do not always tell us whether the goals are correct or whether the presuppositions on which the procedures depend are true. Try this trivial example: if it is true that it is raining, then I shall get wet as I walk home. So the belief that it is raining is submitted to experimental verification. I adopt the procedure of walking home and I actually get wet. But does that in itself prove that it is raining? I could get wet on the way home for a variety of reasons: perhaps someone was watering his lawn and his sprinkler sprayed me, or perhaps it was snowing, or I fell down in a puddle, or some students tried to retaliate for the grades they received by turning a hose on me. That I get wet does not by itself prove the initial belief true. The same experience can be explained with totally different beliefs. To know which belief is true requires more carefully directed observation and a rational evaluation of the alternatives.

The example is overly simplified, but the conclusion is plain: experience alone without rational inquiry is not enough to determine the truth. The experiences of the mystic could be explained on other grounds than those he claims to be true: psychological explanations abound, demonic accounts are sometimes given. It is, of course, possible that some awareness of God is achieved that way, but it would be one devoid of the intelligibility and the scope of truth as well as of the forgiveness we more basically need. Nor could we be sure the experience was of God, without interpretation and rational assessment. Religious experience is by itself no royal road to learning.

Of course, none of this denies that experience matters, or that our truth judgments must take the content of experience into account. The failure of naive empiricism rather underscores the absence of any royal road to learning and poses problems about what role experience should properly play in our reasoning.

# SIX

# How Reliable Is
# Human Reason?

Every schoolboy who has studied geometry knows about deductive reasoning and assumes it is valid, and science students quickly realize how effective inductive methods have been. When we affirm the reliability of human reasoning and explore the contributions of experience, these are the kinds of things we have in mind. The time has come for a closer look.

First, let us take stock of the argument to this point. In chapter one we claimed that truth has its ultimate basis, its unity, and its universality in God, and in chapter two we concluded that no dichotomy of secular and sacred knowledge is allowable. Chapter three then expounded the personal and the propositional aspects of truth, and chapter four argued that while human finiteness and fallenness preclude human infallibility, yet the fact of error does not destroy all possibility of knowing the truth. Chapter five showed that neither faith nor revelation nor experience, for all they do contribute, provide a royal road that bypasses fallible rational processes. We simply cannot avoid reasoning. Knowing and understanding the truth is too valuable to be inhibited by fear of error, and there is no other way to grasp truth than by using the rational powers God created in us. Revelation is a source of knowledge that informs our reasoning, but it is not a substitute for human thought.

To see if reason actually meets our expectations and to be sure of using it aright, we must therefore look more closely at some of the reasoning we employ, and ask what it is like and whether it is in fact as reliable as we have implied. What makes reasoning reliable? What are its limits? Differences exist between reasoning in one area and in another: moral reasoning, historical and scientific explanation, and religious knowledge are not necessarily identical.[1] But our present concern is with the general characteristics of human reasoning rather than with its variations, and with such general characteristics as the discipline of logic describes.

We shall consider two basic methods of reasoning, the deductive and the inductive. There may well be other and less formal kinds of reasoning, but these two will suffice for our purpose. The first kind, deduction, is basic to formal logic and is best exemplified in mathematics. The second, induction, is basic to material logic, which is our reasoning about matters of fact, and has its best-known use in empirical science. While mathematics and empirical science are exemplary for the care and success with which they employ these methods, deduction and induction are also used in philosophical and theological reasoning and many other contexts, and are in fact as basic to the thinking of the man in the street as they are to the scientist or philosopher.

## 1. Deductive reasoning

Our schoolboy who studied geometry knows that if we define certain basic terms and adopt a few basic postulates, we can prove theorem after theorem and develop an entire geometrical system. Analogous attempts have been made to prove theological theses, to develop an entire philosophical system, and to systematize scientific explanations by means of formal logic. Deduction is a common kind of reasoning in any academic field.

In deductive logic the simplest form of argument is the syllogism, in which, as in mathematics, a conclusion follows demonstrably from premises. Logicians since Aristotle have distinguished valid from invalid syllogisms, according to whether a conclusion follows deductively from its premises, for after all even logicians and mathematicians are fallible and have to check on the validity of their proofs. Compare these two simple syllogisms:

(1) All men are mortal.
   Socrates is a man.
   Therefore Socrates is mortal.

---

1. On their differences and similarities, viewed from a Christian perspective, see my *Faith Seeks Understanding* (Eerdmans, 1971).

(2) All men are two-legged.
    All birds are two-legged.
    Therefore all birds are men.

Since syllogism (1) is valid and its premises true, its conclusion also is true; but although the premises of syllogism (2) are true, the conclusion is false because it does not follow from the premises with logical validity. The argument fails to recognize that there may be two unrelated classes of two-legged things. Consider also the following:

(3) All men are four-legged.
    Socrates is a man.
    Therefore Socrates is four-legged.

Here the argument is valid (it has the same form as does (1)), but while the second premise is true, the first premise is false and so the conclusion also is false.

Two conditions are thus necessary in deductive reasoning. The first is illustrated by comparing syllogisms (1) and (2): *the argument must be valid,* or in other words the conclusion must "follow logically" from the relationship between the premises. The second is illustrated by comparing (1) and (3): *the premises must be true.* Deductive reasoning will therefore be successful if we can ensure both logical validity and true premises. Granted these two conditions, all sorts of inferences can be drawn and human knowledge thereby unfolded far beyond what we are aware of initially. Theologians draw inferences from Biblical statements; philosophers draw inferences from presuppositions or from scientific theories; and scientists deduce observable consequences from a hypothesis plus other general information.

(4) Hypothesis: This solution is acid.
    All acids turn litmus red.
    Prediction: Therefore this solution will turn litmus red.

Experimental observation verifies the prediction and so confirms the hypothesis.

Deduction has wide application and works well. But it is not an autonomous form of reasoning, for it depends on two preconditions: rules of valid inference, and the truth of premises. Are they reliable? Are they also ultimately related to God?

    a. *Rules of inference* and the consequently valid forms of the syllogism have been identified by logicians, but the more basic question is this: What makes logical rules binding? What makes valid inferences valid? What is the underlying norm, the basic law that governs reason itself? To what universal and unchanging principle does all deductive reasoning necessarily submit? This basic principle is called the *principle of non-contradiction:* a proposition cannot be both true and false at the same time and in the same respect (i.e., *A* is not non-*A*). This basic principle is tied to the very nature of the truth which reason seeks, for truth and falsity are mutually exclusive. But to say that truth is truth and falsity is not truth is to affirm that *A* is *A* and is not non-*A,* which is the principle of non-contradiction. This principle, which applies to truth itself, must then rule reason's approach to truth. I cannot possibly speak contradictions and thereby speak the truth. Reason itself does not rule except so far as it is ruled by truth.

By way of illustration, consider our previous syllogism (2) about men and birds: the premises indicate two different classes of two-legged creatures, which the conclusion mistakenly identifies. It is a mistake because the first premise means only that men constitute one class of two-legged things, not the *whole* class of two-legged things. To make one class into the whole class, when it is not true that it is the whole class, is to affirm falsehood instead of truth. *A* would be non-*A*. To give us a valid argument, the first premise must address the whole class of two-legged creatures, of which the second premise addresses a part. Thus, syllogism (2) would have to read:

(2a)  All two-legged creatures are men. (False)
       All birds are two-legged creatures.
       Therefore all birds are men.

But then the false first premise produces a false conclusion.

The law of non-contradiction, related as it is to the distinction between truth and falsehood, is basic to all deductive reasoning. Rules of valid inference are simply applications of it. Attempts have been made to argue that it is a logically necessary principle: either we affirm the law of non-contradiction or we deny it. But to deny it we must affirm it, for the law I deny (*A*) is still the law I deny (i.e., *A* is *A*) rather than not the law I deny (i.e., *A* is not non-*A*). Since I cannot deny the law without affirming it, to deny it is therefore self-contradictory and logically impossible. Thus, the law is logically necessary and universally binding.

The difficulty with this argument, of course, is its circularity: it assumes the very thing it seeks to prove, namely that logically we cannot contradict ourselves by both affirming and denying $A$. It says that if we want to be logical, as defined by the principle of non-contradiction, we have to abide by the principle of non-contradiction. Admittedly so, but that assumes we want to be logical as so defined. If we do, then in practice we must obey that logical principle. This exhibits the *practical necessity* of the principle, but it does not demonstrate its autonomous *logical necessity* independently of the practical desire to be logical. Nor do I think it possible to demonstrate its logical necessity independently of other considerations, both practical and theoretical. The necessity of the principle, I suggest, stems from the fact that in God's world, the world in which we live and think, true is true and false is false, so that if we want truth we must in practice hold to the principle of non-contradiction.

Some philosophers, equally dissatisfied with the argument about logical necessity and the appeal to practical necessity, revert instead to prior questions about the meaning of language. They claim that the principle of non-contradiction is simply a rule against meaningless discourse. In making an assertion ("all men are two-legged") we apply a term ("two-legged") to things ("men") we take, truly or falsely, to be real. When we violate the principle of non-contradiction we both apply and do not apply the term "two-legged" to "men," and what we say accordingly has no meaning.

I have no objection to this as it stands, unless one adds that the principle of non-contradiction is *only* a rule of language, and is thereby arbitrary or relative. A rule governing assertions about reality says something about truth and reality as well as about language and reasoning. In fact as well as in language, $A$ is not non-$A$. And this is finally so because God made it so, and because God himself is God and not non-God.

We have said, then, that the nature of valid inference is tied to the nature of truth and reality, but we may add that if the nature of truth and reality derives from God then the nature of valid inference also ultimately derives from God, who is who he is, who cannot contradict himself, and for whom true is true. It derives from God and his unchanging fidelity. This immediately answers any concern the Christian may have about the reliability of human reason and of deductive logic in particular. If human reasoning depends on the law of non-contradiction, if the law of non-contradiction is tied to the nature of truth and reality, and if the nature of truth and reality depends on God, then human reasoning depends on God. Accordingly, we can trust reasoning and safeguard against what is false by following the rules of valid inference. The way to avoid error is not to avoid reasoning (if that were even possible) but to improve reasoning. This suggests the value of a good course in logic and the continued intellectual discipline it takes to reason logically.

One difficulty remains, which affects not the nature and basis of deductive reasoning which we have just discussed but rather its applicability and usefulness. According to the law of non-contradiction, *A* is *A* and not non-*A* *at the same time and in the same respect*. The principle applies in other words to that which does not change, so that deduction is a logic of the unchanging. The German philosopher Hegel argued that since all finite existence is historical and constantly subject to change, the law of non-contradiction is therefore trivial. In time, *A* becomes non-*A*, even though at any one point in time *A* is not non-*A*. A baby is not an adult, but in the course of time he becomes one. Renaissance art is not Enlightenment art, but in the course of time it gives place to and becomes engulfed by it. The logic of historical and temporal processes, according to Hegel, is not deductive but dialectical: it moves through the conflict and interpenetration of opposites (thesis and antithesis) to an emergent synthesis that both preserves and transcends the opposites that produce it.

Hegel's point is not that the traditional laws of logic are mistaken and that no distinction between true and false remains (as some writers have wrongly assumed), but that deductive logic has limited use. It is a logic of the eternal, not the temporal. It requires that we arrest the current of history in midstream by thinking in abstraction from the processes of time. But this does not render logic powerless either in mathematics or in science or in philosophy. There *are* unchanging structures that time either does not change at all or does not alter in some significant respect, unchanging characteristics of human nature and of the world around us, for instance, and the unchanging nature and revelation of God. Deduction may be difficult to apply to particular historical events, and Hegel rightly objects to attempts to pour concrete historical processes into such logical molds, as was admittedly done in his day. But that simply limits the range of application of deductive logic and is a far cry from claiming that the law of non-contradiction can be ignored or that the irrational now rules. On the contrary, reason is trustworthy as long as it obeys the law of non-contradiction with its emphasis on "the same time and respect," and as long as deductive structures of thought are not superimposed where they may not belong.

b. *The premises* in deductive reasoning require further consideration. In order to secure a true conclusion it is essential (1) that the premises extend universally, to the entire class under consideration, and (2) that the premises be true.

The first of these conditions is illustrated by our previous syllogism:

(2) All men are two-legged.
All birds are two-legged.
Therefore all birds are men.

On the surface the two premises may seem universally extended or "distributed," but this is only the case for their subject-terms ("all men" and "all birds"), not for their predicates. Yet the predicates provide a common middle term ("two-legged") to link the premises together, a term which is not universally extended in either premise: in each case it refers to a part and not the whole of the class of two-legged things. All men constitute one part of that class, and all birds constitute another part. One can only draw an inference from premises whose middle term is universally extended to include the whole class, as in the following example where the middle term is "all men":

(1) All men are mortal.
Socrates is a man.
Therefore Socrates is mortal.

Similarly with the middle term "acid" in:

(4) This solution is acid.
All acids turn litmus red.
Therefore this solution will turn litmus red.

The middle terms "men" and "acid" are each universally extended in one premise. Otherwise no logical connection would exist between the premises, and no conclusion would validly follow. For syllogistic reasoning to be trustworthy, therefore, we must know something that is universal as well as true.

Immediately a limitation arises. As Søren Kierkegaard pointed out, we can draw no logical conclusions from what is unique rather than universally alike. Yet there is something unique about each human individual and his decisions. Consequently, no complete system of syllogisms that covers all existence can ever be constructed, unless perhaps by an omniscient God. Abstract logical systems are possible, says Kierkegaard—many alternative systems indeed are possible—but an existential system that embraces all the unique aspects of our existence is humanly impossible.

A further example, which is of current theological importance, is the relation between a unique historical event, such as the resurrection of Jesus, and its meaning for theology and for our redemption. If Jesus' resurrection is a unique act of God, *sui generis* (that is, the one and only member of the whole class), then no logically necessary inferences follow about its theological meaning. There is a logical gap between

(i) Jesus rose from the dead

and (ii) God raised him for our justification.

The truth of neither (i) nor (ii) is in question here, but rather that the truth of (ii) cannot be logically proved on the basis of (i) alone. We cannot *prove* that the Biblical writers drew correct implications from the events they recorded, that what they teach about the meaning of Christ's resurrection necessarily follows from the resurrection itself, because we cannot use deductive reasoning unless there are at least two premises with a universally extended middle term. This limitation of logic explains how existential theologians can reinterpret Biblical events and "demythologize" the interpretation recorded in Scripture, for no statement about the unique can extend to other members of the class (there are none), so as to allow valid inferences. It seems that the Biblical relation of the event to its meaning was somehow learned from God's revelation or otherwise adduced, not inferred by deductive reasoning alone.

Premises must be both universally extended and true. But from where can we obtain such premises? Two sources of knowledge must be considered, the one independent of and the other dependent on experience. The first is usually called a priori knowledge and the second is empirical knowledge.

*A priori knowledge* has been claimed by rationalists like Plato and Descartes, who hold that truth is directly apprehended after we sift erroneous and dubious conceptions out of all the ideas that come to mind. This intellectual sifting process has been variously labelled "dialectic" and "analysis," and the resultant a priori knowledge has been variously identified as "innate," "intuitive," or "self-evident." Descartes likened it to the intuitive truth of axioms in Euclidean geometry.

The problem with this claim is pointed up by the fact that what Euclid took to be axiomatic and universally true, modern geometricians recognize to be simply the postulates of one geometry as distinct from others. Non-Euclidean geometries substitute some other postulates for Euclid's fifth axiom about parallel straight lines, and the results have immense value both in mathematics and science. Similarly in other areas, truths that one generation held to be self-evident (such as the individual's right to life, liberty, and the pursuit of happiness) were far from self-evident to earlier generations and may be rejected in later theories. Some God-given and universal human rights may exist, but this is something political theory has to argue in the face of other premises about God and man and society, premises which likewise are not universally accepted. At some time or other almost every Western moral or religious belief has been called self-evident, only to be challenged by those who find them far from evident.

I myself am inclined to the view that few if any truths are strictly speaking self-evident intuitions apart from tautologies, analytic statements, and purely "logical truths" that simply embody the form of basic logical principles like that of non-contradiction. This includes mathematical statements whose truth is universal and necessary provided we grant the definitions and postulates of the mathematical system in question. $3 + 4 = 7$ is necessarily true in a "base ten" number system, but in a "base five" system $3 + 4 = 12$. Such mathematical truths are "system dependent," and self-evident only within the system of which they are part, and not independently.

There is another sense of *a priori* knowledge in which it refers not to self-evident intuitions *per se* but to innate ideas. In this sense all human beings are equipped with truths that could not be drawn from experience. Some people suppose the idea of God to be universally innate, and take Romans 1:19 to support that view: "that which may be known of God is manifest *in* them." But the

Greek preposition translated "in" can also be rendered "to" or even "among," depending on the context. In this case the context plainly speaks of the witness of creation to the existence and greatness of God, and of man's consequent moral responsibility. So the translation "*to* them" (RSV) seems appropriate.[2]

John Calvin, in the opening chapters of his *Institutes of the Christian Religion,* explains that apart from special revelation men gain an idea of God because of the witness of creation and the correlated witness of man's own nature, itself part of the creation. Created in God's image, man bears in himself the seed of religion (*semen religionis*). It is purely germinal, however, a potential for becoming religious rather than an innate idea. With the witness of creation around him, man acquires some sense of a deity (*sensus deitatis*), not a clear conception of the Judaeo-Christian God but some awareness of a vaguely conceived supreme being. This religious awareness is sufficient to hold him accountable (as in Romans 1), but it needs to be informed by Scripture before it is sufficient for faith and practice.

This kind of approach to the idea of God seems consonant with what anthropology and comparative religion indicate of the vast variations in man's religious beliefs. That God-concepts and God-substitutes develop indicates only a significant kind of intellectual and personal need in all men, not a universally innate knowledge. The same conclusion may be applied to other supposedly innate ideas, so that while universal moral obligations are not known innately (as Plato and Augustine seem to have thought), yet the nature of man is such that in practice he needs and develops a concept of justice, for instance, and he relates that concept to his physical life and safety, to sex and marriage, to property, and to the social and political order.

The development of our ideas, then, seems mostly due to our needs and purposes and experiences in the kind of world God created. But man and his world are not just physical things; man is also a social being, so that ideas develop in and are transmitted through societal relations. This development and transmission of ideas explains both the similarities and the diversities of human

---

2. I have not here dealt with such views of the a priori as Kant's or Quine's: their problem is still to establish indubitable a priori truths as premises for deductive reasoning.

belief more adequately than do theories of innate or self-evident knowledge.

It follows that most or all of the premises we use in deductive reasoning are either adapted or adopted from some source (whether from Scripture or current assumptions or whatever), or else depend more directly on experience. To derive universally extended premises from experience is the work of inductive reasoning, not intuition or deduction. To decide the truth of such empirical statements is the task of material logic.

## 2. Inductive reasoning

a. *The principle of induction.* Among the difficulties confronting empirical knowledge is the incompleteness of human experience. Further observation of anything is possible while I and it both last. This is the case with a thing as simple as the ballpoint pen that was presented to me in a desk set some years ago; I have valued it, examined it, taken it apart, replaced the refill again and again, put it together, chewed on it, and so forth. Yet my experience of it is still incomplete. I could put it under a microscope, run various chemical tests on its body, see how it responds to heat and extreme cold, undertake comparative studies with other pens of the same make and with pens of different makes, and do statistical studies on the longevity of each successive refill. I could examine it as a scientist sees it, or I could see it as a shapely art object, well proportioned and with shining lines of reflected light slicing through its blackness. I could see it as a child might see it, viewing my miniature face reflected in its shiny surface, lovingly stroking its smoothness, admiring its black body, and dreaming of things it says and does and of the stories it tells. But my experience of it still remains incomplete.

Our best empirical descriptions are "progress reports" and not, strictly speaking, "conclusions" in the sense that nothing further can be said. My awareness of a particular thing, event, or person is always incomplete and always subject to possible amendment. Only my purposes in examining it determine when I have gone far enough.

Empirical generalizations are additionally precarious because they apply to a whole class of things, of which I may have examined only a small sample. Inductive reasoning, therefore, presupposes the uniformity of the part with the whole, and that is something which induction itself cannot prove.

Similarly scientific predictions of what will happen in a certain experiment or under other given circumstances are only possible if we assume that future and past experiences will be uniform, yet the uniformity of neither all of nature nor all of experience can be demonstrated from within the limits of our experience to date. Deductive logic needs to establish the truth of universally extended premises, but this is impossible on the basis of limited experience unless we assume as one of our premises the uniformity of that part with all possible experience.

We need what is called a *principle of induction* to make inductive generalization possible, a principle that can rule inductive reasoning just as the principle of non-contradiction rules deductive reasoning. On it depend the inductive and experimental methods of science, the rules of empirical evidence, and the very possibility of a material logic.

David Hume stated the problem bluntly. On the one hand, if we look to future experience to justify induction, we are using induction to justify itself and this is circular. In addition, experience can never produce more than a progress report about the uniformity of experience "thus far": even though "thus far" keeps moving further along, an unexperienced and unknown future always looms ahead to frustrate our certainties. On the other hand, if we use deduction and try to infer the principle of induction from something else we know, then we face the old difficulty of establishing universally extended premises that are not known a priori. At best we will, like J. S. Mill, deduce the principle of induction from an empirical generalization about the uniformity of nature or experience, but that too is circular. How can we know empirically the uniformity of all nature? How then can we establish the principle of induction on which material logic depends?

Hume suggested that we *believe* in the uniformity of nature without proving it to be true, because the regularities of past experience create mental habits and elicit feelings which we cannot avoid. He saw this as nature's way of coordinating human belief with the world in which we live, a way that has its parallels in the instinctive behavior of animals. On this account, acceptance of the principle of induction stems not from rational argument but from the psychological processes that unthinkingly incite belief and condition everyday practice.

Bertrand Russell wrestled with this problem for years, and finally agreed in his *Human Knowledge: Its Scope and Limits* that the principle of induction is not established either deductively or inductively; yet since the postulates it involves work so effectively in explaining the success of science and technology, we may justifiably accept them for all empirical knowledge. This, he frankly admits, means that *purely* empirical knowledge is impossible.

It appears, then, that inductive reasoning is no more autonomous than is deductive reasoning, for they depend alike on our acceptance of the underlying principles that make them possible. Those underlying principles cannot be proved binding without circular arguments, but depend rather on the purposes of reasoning. As the principle of non-contradiction depends on the practical demands of speaking meaningfully or of seeking the true rather than the false, so the principle of induction and the assumption of nature's uniformity depend on the practical necessity of generalizing, or of predicting and planning for future experience. They are, then, matters of practical necessity.

The Christian will not meet this conclusion with alarm. Both his view of truth and reality (and so of non-contradiction) and his view of the uniformity of nature (and so of induction) are related to his belief in God.[3] Belief in the orderliness of nature, and the hope that with experience we can live and think and act effectively in this world, depend on belief in a wise and faithful creator. In God's world and thanks to God, inductive reasoning is trustworthy as long as we employ inductive methods which, like scientific experimentation, allow for self-correction, and as long as we guard against inductive fallacies like hasty generalization and poor sampling techniques. To avoid error we need not avoid inductive reasoning or scientific inquiry; rather we need to gain and to practice intellectual discipline and to be logically careful, and we need the honesty to correct our mistakes. A good course in inductive logic and scientific method might contribute.

b. *Are we sure of our facts?* The trustworthiness of inductive reasoning depends not only on the principle of induction but also

---

3. Other world-views of course support these principles on their own presuppositions. I am not claiming that *only* theism offers any systematic support.

on the empirical information which it employs. Here as in other aspects of human knowledge we often take it for granted that the facts of experience are indubitable, incorrigible, and universally the same. Empiricists (who hold that all knowledge derives from experience) sometimes speak of sense data in that way, and Bertrand Russell regarded "knowledge by acquaintance" as the bedrock of all empirical knowledge. Two difficulties challenge this assumption: the relativity of perception and the interpretive nature of perceptual activity.

The relativity of perception has haunted philosophers from before Plato to the present day. How particular things appear to me and the sense data I have as I look at them depend on a variety of observation conditions, both objective and subjective. They depend on which side of the object is towards me, on how its texture reflects the light, on the color and intensity of illumination, and on the condition of my eyes. Subjectively they depend on the attention I give, on what I expect to see and therefore on what I read into the present experience, on the purpose for which I examine things, on how careful an observer I am, and so forth. These factors apply only to seeing; parallel variables apply to the other four senses. In addition the object itself may be moving or growing or changing in color or some other quality. Perceptual conditions are thus relative and not universally the same. Nor is our perception indubitable or incorrigible; if we allow for changing circumstances and conditions, it yields at best beliefs that are sufficient for practical purposes.

The same conclusion is underscored when we consider how a scientific description of, say, a wooden table differs from ordinary observation. Both accounts are supposedly empirical, yet while an ordinary observer finds it smooth and rectangular and reddish-brown and utterly solid, the scientific description talks of the relative density of its materials or of particles buzzing around in all directions to give it a certain molecular structure. The two accounts are of course relative to their methods and instruments and practical purposes. With this in mind, what we call "facts of experience" are really human observations relative to all the conditions that make those observations possible.

To be sure of our facts we try to limit the variables, we emphasize the repeatability and the public character of our data, and we question findings that are incongruous with what was previously accepted. For most purposes this is often sufficient. In most of ordinary life we can trust our senses, and when we do make mistakes further experience corrects us. Yet it remains that a fact of experience is not isolatable and independent, but is contingent on a whole web of circumstances with which it is intricately interwoven.

Another way of stating this is that we have no "bare facts," only "perceived facts" in relation to our present purposes and observation conditions. These are not bare facts but "inter-prefacts." Consciously or unconsciously, experience involves various kinds of interpretation. There are causal interpretations uncovering the factors that produce what we observe; there are motivational and purposive interpretations that explain why people appear to act as they do; there are "general law" interpretations that treat particular phenomena as examples of previous empirical generalizations; there are valuations that interpret the moral or aesthetic or intellectual worth of experiences. But each kind of interpretation brings to experience its own interpretive principle: namely cause and effect; or a conception of human motivation and purpose that has implications about freedom and values; or a uniformity principle that permits generalizations; or a set of values. Experience is not self-interpreting, for we bring interpretations to experience and try them on for fit, rather than reading them straight off the "facts."

Consider the following:

(1) He stole that pen.
(2) You made him do it.
(3) He ought to be punished.

(1) includes an interpretive term, "stole," which loads the facts with moral connotations and invokes ethical judgment. (2) not only implies a moral judgment about those who induce others to steal, but it also introduces a concept of causation that has implications regarding freedom and responsibility. (3) invokes the idea of social obligation, a tacit concept of justice and a theory of punishment. Even an observation like

(4) That shirt is yellow

is not purely empirical, for it is about a material object (which is more than any finite set of observations yields) and it presupposes observation conditions that are necessary for the shirt to look yellow as it does.

The outcome is that we know no facts independently of observers and observation conditions. It is a *fact* that it is raining at time $t$ and place $p$, but not independently of such conditions. It is also a *fact of experience* in that an observer notices it because it affects him personally (e.g., he gets wet) or it bears on his purposes and values (e.g., he was about to go out with his girl friend).

Observation conditions merit a little more attention, because they bear a striking similarity to the rider in the principle of non-contradiction: "at the same time and in the same respect." A fact is the fact it is and not something else *at a given time and place and in other given respects*. The similarity is clear. It seems that the possibility of identifying objective facts and of using them in inductive reasoning rests on the principle of non-contradiction. If that principle holds, we can speak meaningfully of objective facts which are what they are "at the same time and in the same respect," whether I know them or not.

Inductive reasoning is in general possible because of the principle of induction. It is in practice trustworthy within the limits of what we mean by "facts of experience," that is to say within the limits set by (a) the principle of non-contradiction and (b) the purposes and perceptions of the observer. It will accordingly be safeguarded by careful methods that focus on (a) what occurs at time $t$ and place $p$, etc., in relation to (b) the purposes of the observer. This of course is what careful scientific and inductive methods are all about, and it is their safeguards that help make empirical reasoning reliable.

## 3. Knowledge as justified belief

We have discussed deductive and inductive reasoning, but it appears that we bring to such reasoning more than logic and empirical data: we bring interpretative principles. Recent studies of scientific knowledge have argued that observation is "theory laden," and that science employs models as guiding images in generating its hypotheses and developing its theories.[4] The mechanistic cause-effect model, for example, lies behind both

---

4. See T. S. Kuhn, *The Structure of Scientific Revolutions* (U. of Chicago, 1962); Norwood Hanson, *Patterns of Discovery* (Cambridge, 1958); and Stephen Toulmin, *Foresight and Understanding* (Hutchinson Univ. Library, 1961).

Newton's theory of gravitation and behavioristic explanations of human conduct. By virtue of the model, no consideration of purpose figures in its account of either nature or man.

A theory is taken to be true because of its explanatory power, retrodictively concerning the past and predictively concerning the future. Yet theories are open to revision and so are models. Sometimes crucial experiments or accumulated experience elicit changes; sometimes a scientist's imagination adduces alternative ways of thinking about what occurs. The point is that our reasoning interprets what is given. Yet the human mind is not free to think what it will, for good science is obedient to the truth and must respect the controls that both the data and sound logic exercise in theory-formation. Alternative explanations may well be admissible, but not "any old theory" will do. Explanations and theories are subject to careful scrutiny and in need of verification. And what is true of science in these regards is true of explanations and theories in other disciplines too.

What conclusion can we then draw? Is human reason trustworthy? Within limits and with qualifications. We must regard knowledge not as logically conclusive and incorrigibly certain, but rather as belief that for its own purposes is rationally justified. It is justified in practice (viz., for its own purposes), even when some theoretical difficulties remain, as long as it rests on good reasoning.

The practical justification of belief is familiar to those who have read Hume or Kant or Cardinal Newman's *Grammar of Assent,* or more recent work like William James' essay "The Will to Believe" or the writings of common sense philosophers like G. E. Moore. Although conclusive logical demonstrations are not always possible and *theoretical* doubt is therefore possible, the evidence we have and the basic principles of reasoning combine with the practical demands of life and thought to thoroughly justify certain beliefs.

Human reasoning is after all a part of how human nature and existence are geared to the demands and the purposes of life. Human reasoning is an effective part of God's creation, but it is neither autonomous nor self-justifying. *For practical purposes,* the purposes of life and faith and learning, confidence in human reason is well grounded. The basic principles of non-contradiction and of induction are universal and necessary for the purposes of human thought, even if they are not independently and logically necessary. Good reasoning will therefore adopt the rules and procedures those principles require. The result is not that reason can prove everything, but that we can know some things even though we "know in part" and "see through a glass darkly." It is not surprising that we should find deductive reasoning effective and wonder at the knowledge explosion that scientific methods have facilitated. If we understand why this is so, we will thank God for it all and will be more diligent in our own intellectual development and activity.

# SEVEN

# On Justifying Our Beliefs

Time and time again the question arises, whether we are discussing the latest international news or another political scandal. In courts of law, the fate of people depends on it. In the marketplace of ideas where the claims of Christianity confront every other conceivable belief, it poses the basic question for Christian apologetics. No university student can long avoid asking the question: How do you know it's true?

So far our discussion has been about the nature and basis of truth and of human knowledge. But that is not enough. Every discussion of truth turns eventually to criteria by which we may test the truth of what we hear or believe. Philosophers have spoken of a correspondence test for truth that looks for a one-to-one correlation between propositions and the objective facts they purport to represent. This may be fine for statements like "It is now raining in London," but it hardly helps with "Stealing is wrong," or "God is a spirit, infinite in wisdom, goodness, love, and power." The correspondence to reality of these assertions is hard to ascertain by empirical means at least. Other tests have therefore been introduced, such as the rational coherence of a proposition with the body of already accepted and assured beliefs, so that we know stealing is wrong because it follows logically from other knowledge we have; or the pragmatic procedure of determining whether acting on a belief actually secures the practical results it implies, so that the belief that stealing is wrong is borne out by what happens as a result of somebody's thievery.

Each of these traditional tests has much-advertised difficulties that can be read about in introductory philosophy textbooks. One difficulty is that the tests must be appropriate to the nature of truth, so that the pragmatist tests truth as he conceives it: the workability or cash value of a belief in a given practical situation.

But if truth means something more or something other than this, we must test for the more or the other rather than settling for something situational and pragmatic alone. The correspondence test of truth is characteristically empiricist, while the coherence test fits the demands of a more rationalistic epistemology. This is not to say that these tests have no adaptability outside their native habitats, but that we must be careful to match the tests to the nature of truth as we conceive it; otherwise we end up testing for something other or less than we really want.

Our point of departure must accordingly be our understanding of the nature of truth. Let us then remind ourselves that truth is universal and unchanging and ultimately one. Our test or tests must look for these characteristics in whatever purports to be true. Moreover, truth has both a cognitive and a more fully personal side. So too does knowledge; it is not a purely detached matter but a genuinely personal involvement. To "know the truth" is not to hold it with a purely objective attitude on the basis of logically demonstrable proofs, but something far more personal than this. "You shall know the truth, and the truth shall make you free" (John 8:32) points up man's close personal relation to truth. Our tests must therefore consider this relationship, for it is *we* who make truth-judgments, *we* who believe, *we* who affirm this or that and commit ourselves in the process. If it is *our* knowledge-claims that bear witness to the truth, then they should contain evidence not only of what is universal and unchanging and unified, but also of what we can most fully appreciate and respond to as human beings.

Let me put this another way. We have parted company with the Enlightenment claim that man, his beliefs and his actions, can both rule and be ruled by objective reason alone. The rule of reason in the realm of morals and politics was properly criticized by Augustine in ancient times, and David Hume in the eighteenth century added criticisms of the rule of reason alone in the realm of belief. The same realism about man that undermines the rule of reason in ethics and politics also undermines its power by itself to justify beliefs. Objective reasons alone do not control man's actions; neither do they control his beliefs. If we are to control what we allow ourselves to believe or do, if we want to justify any beliefs or actions at all, then we must see more clearly what in us does in fact control human belief and action. Belief and action, it will appear, are controlled by a combination of objectively rational considerations on the one hand, and by more subjective and personal considerations on the other.

Some older writers viewed man and his beliefs in terms of faculty psychology with its three separate faculties of intellect, will, and emotion. On this account belief is an act of the will and, according to David Hume at least, it is more influenced by emotion than intellect. I prefer to think of belief as a whole-personal condition, not an act of intellect alone or will alone.[1]

We must, then, be clear about the nature of a person, for it is persons who believe. The human person is (1) a rational being, (2) a valuing being, and (3) an agent who acts. These are cumulative characteristics in that the most inclusive thing we can say about man is that he is, in all else, a responsible agent. But as an agent he is also a valuing being, for he acts purposefully in pursuit of his values. As a valuing being who acts he is also a rational being, for value judgments require that we conceive of what is good and have reasons for acting as we do. Reasoning is thus part of the action, not detached from it, not value free, nor the whole of life. Thinking is rather a function of living than life is a function of impersonal thought.

As a rational being a man examines evidence and arguments and brings them to bear both on what he values and on what is proposed to his belief and action. As a valuing being he is motivated not only by what he knows but also by what he loves. If a man really loves the truth, this will direct his thinking, but if not he is likely to prostitute both knowledge and truth to lesser and more selfish ends. His values help to shape his beliefs. As a personal agent man believes in order to act. He has many particular projects in life that require him to formulate and justify beliefs, as well as the overall project of life itself which he struggles to understand in order to live with meaning and purpose. His

---

1. In this I reflect post-Kantian emphases on the primacy of practical over theoretical reason, seen not only in Kant but also in pragmatists like William James and existential philosophers like Merleau-Ponty and Martin Heidegger. In British philosophy it is evident in the appeal to ordinary uses of language and in recent philosophy of human action. Along different lines it appears in writers like John Macmurray whose *The Self as Agent* (Faber & Faber, 1957) argues more fully than I can here. Some of the theological possibilities of Macmurray's approach are evident in Robert Blaikie, *"Secular Christianity" and the God Who Acts* (Eerdmans, 1970).

projects determine what knowledge he seeks and what degree of certainty is needed for belief and action.

This account of what man is bears on the justification of belief in that we can now formulate procedures related not only to the universality and unity of truth, but also to our personal involvement with truth. Some philosophers who recognize the person-dependent nature of belief still offer only rational controls; others offer only pragmatic or existential justifications of belief. Because of the personal nature of truth and knowledge, and because of the unitary nature of the human person, we must keep the more fully personal considerations tied to the rational, as in fact they appear to be in the responsible conduct of daily life.

The following scheme now falls into place:

(1) Man is a rational being. Reasoning is concerned both with the facts of experience (as in induction) and with the logical relations of ideas (as in deduction). We therefore need (a) an empirical test, which we shall label "empirical adequacy" rather than using the older term "correspondence," and (b) a more formal test which we label "rational coherence."

(2) Man is a valuing being whose values influence his beliefs. In order to get at the universality of truth we must therefore ask what is universal and unchanging in human values; otherwise we risk allowing all our beliefs to become as relative as are some of our culturally and individually relative values. We must also keep in mind that values are not simply emotive reactions: they are cognitive as well as emotive, and so are amenable to rational assessment.

(3) Man is an agent who acts and whose action-projects require beliefs. Here too we must ask what is universal and unchanging, what projects are universal, and what is the most inclusive project that gives unified direction to all else we do.

We shall pursue each of these directions in what follows, looking for ways in which they bear witness to the universality and unity of truth. Inevitably, it is a somewhat difficult and more technical subject than much of what has gone before, but then no guarantees were given that the quest for truth would be easy. There is still no royal road to learning.

## 1. Rational assessments of belief

a. *Empirical adequacy.* A number of contemporary writers hold that three conditions must be fulfilled if we are to say "I know": "I know *p*" implies

(1) I believe that *p*,
(2) *p* is true,
(3) I have adequate evidence for *p*.

These conditions have been extensively criticized, especially the second, for I cannot say "*p* is true" unless I already know *p*. But our concern is with the third condition about having "adequate evidence" to justify the claim to know *p*. Adequacy, we noted in previous chapters, does not imply conclusive proof or logically final guarantees. It is rather adequate *to authorize* or *justify* belief, to make it an intellectually honest and morally responsible act, to provide whatever degree of assurance is necessary for the practical purposes of this particular belief.

Evidently then, "adequacy" requires consideration of the values and projects that involved us in knowing *p*. But if for the moment we bracket those more personal aspects of truth, we can still ask when the evidence is *rationally* adequate. To answer this question, we restate the third condition for saying "I know *p*":

(3a) *p* follows logically from the evidence.

To follow logically is to follow according to universal laws of logic discussed in chapter six: either of inductive logic rooted in the principle of induction, or of deductive logic rooted in the principle of non-contradiction. We shall say more about the latter in considering rational coherence as a test. According to the former, inductive logic, "adequate" evidence will always be incomplete but must still be sufficiently representative of the whole to justify inductive generalizations. We must consequently face squarely all available evidence and tailor our conclusions to the evidence rather than vice versa.

Adequacy, then, means there is a *sufficient scope* of evidence to bear witness to the whole. At times the Western mind has tended to consider only scientific sorts of evidence, assuming that unscientific observers are unreliable or that other than sensory experience is irrelevant to the truth. But these tactics are self-defeating because they arbitrarily narrow the scope of admissible evidence. Moral, aesthetic, social, historical, and religious experience must all be accounted for, as well as scientific evidence. Insofar as they exhibit universal traits, they too bear witness to the truth. The empirical adequacy of any world-view, whether theism or naturalism or whatever, depends on its being able to embrace universal aspects of all kinds of human experience.

But more than "scope" is needed. *Good fit* is also essential, because it is possible that a belief might take account of an experience but push it out of shape, distort its natural import, smother it with other input, and refuse to let it speak. The Freudian explanation of religious belief strikes me as a case in point. It seems to have empirical scope, but it has to twist religious experience artificially and silence some of its unique sounds in order to fit it into the theory.

The analogy of good fit is drawn from the fit of a shoe: it (the belief) must neither cramp nor distort the foot (the evidence) nor be so loose that the foot can neither control it nor wrinkle it into its final shape. The greater the scope of evidence and the better the fit of a belief, the greater becomes its empirical adequacy and so its justification.

Empirical adequacy is strengthened when $p$ not only follows logically from the evidence (3a) but also when a further condition pertains:

(4)  The evidence is open to repeated examination, or at least is public.

Natural scientists speak of *repeatable* evidence, but that is not strictly possible with historical and some other beliefs. The condition of *public* evidence, therefore, recognizes that the case for belief $p$ is strengthened if it can be investigated by other people at other times and in other situations. We can invoke intersubjective checks to offset the possibility of one individual or a few distorting the case or begging the question.

The public character of the evidence for the resurrection of Jesus Christ is a good example. For all the popular hymn says ("You ask me how I know he lives, he lives within my heart"), the strongest evidence lies in public historical data rather than in private religious experience. The Christian belief in Christ's resurrection is supported by public evidence: an empty tomb, guards who were punished, and successive resurrection appearances that changed the lives of the disciples and the direction of history.

Of course, people continue to disagree, for belief not only rests on evidence but is also person-dependent, influenced by the values we hold and the projects we pursue. The man who sets out from naturalistic presuppositions to argue against a historical resurrection of Christ is less likely to conclude by believing than one who is already a theist attracted to the person of Jesus. The very project on which he has embarked, and the values which led him to the task, will influence what he finds believable. Consequently, honesty and objectivity require that we keep our values and projects under scrutiny in the process of justifying belief. But thus far we have seen that empirical adequacy depends on (a) universal laws of logic, (b) universal aspects of experience, and (c) intersubjective checks. These help us transcend our individual limitations towards what is universally true.

b. *Rational coherence*. If the truth we seek is ultimately unified, the justification of our beliefs calls for evidence of such unity. Two complementary approaches are possible, (1) negative and (2) positive.

(1) The negative approach employs the logical principle of *non-contradiction* in order to avoid any logical inconsistency, either of a given belief or within the whole body of what we believe. The principle of non-contradiction, it will be recalled, affirms that a proposition and its contradictory cannot both be true at the same time and in the same respect. A self-contradictory proposition is necessarily false, and a proposed belief which contradicts one or more of a previously established set of beliefs is likewise unacceptable.

The problem of evil has traditionally been posed for theism on this basis. It is argued that the occurrence of evils which serve no good purpose is logically inconsistent with the belief that God is infinite in wisdom, goodness, and power. Such a God would know how to overcome evil, would want to do it, and would be capable of doing so. At least one of the following is therefore said to be the case: either the most radical evil ultimately serves a good purpose, or God does not know what to do about it and so is not infinitely wise, or God does not care and so is not infinitely good, or God has not been able to succeed against evil and so is not infinitely powerful. Some conclude that God is limited in power, while others conclude by doubting the very existence of a

God with such personal attributes as wisdom, goodness, and power.

But to claim that evil poses a logical contradiction for theism is more like calling "check" than "checkmate." It challenges us to find a logical move that can avoid the apparent contradiction, and Christians have not lacked further logical moves.[2] They have argued that the most radical evil ultimately serves a good and wise purpose, that we have adequate evidence of God's wisdom, goodness, and power, and that God has already acted to overcome evil. While conclusive empirical verification of the triumph of good over evil awaits the future, a rationally coherent account of evil can be given now that is consistent with Biblical theism.

In some cases the initial inconsistency may not be immediately resolved. It may take several complex moves to escape the challenge, for the beliefs involved may be such that their logical interrelations cannot be sorted out in one move. In religious belief, especially, the subject matter remains shrouded in mystery, is only partially revealed, and has to be probed with slow and painstaking steps. Frequently, tensions become evident within one's beliefs: the tension between the disciplinary value of evil and its demonic character, between freedom and determinism, between the immanence of God's activity and his eternal transcendence, between the changing and the unchanging, between what is and what ought to be. As long as we "know in part" and "see through a glass darkly," we have difficulty being completely sure in all cases whether we have satisfactorily resolved the tension within our beliefs and moved out of "check."

Consequently, while spotting a contradiction furthers the examination of a position, it can result either in a relatively minor readjustment and restatement, or in the introduction of additional factors that have not hitherto been brought into play—all of which fall short of a conclusive "checkmate" that ends the game. The procedure of locating apparent contradictions is helpful but inconclusive. If in the final analysis a belief remains inconsistent with whatever else we know to be true, it must be false. But if it is consistent, that does not establish its truth; it simply shows that the belief is logically possible.

---

2. See Hugh Sylvester, *Arguing with God* (Inter-Varsity Press, 1971); C.S. Lewis, *The Problem of Pain* (Geoffrey Bles, 1940); and George Mavrodes, *Belief in God* (Random House, 1970), chapter four.

I called this a *negative* procedure. A proposition may be logically consistent with other beliefs, yet still be false. Consider the following:

(1) Today it is raining.

(2) It is now October.

(3) The temperature is 70° Fahrenheit.

None of these statements logically contradicts the others as would

(4) The temperature is 10° below zero.

Yet that does not establish their truth. The fact is that it is now April, not October, and the temperature is closer to 40° than 70°. Non-contradiction or logical consistency is a negative, not a positive criterion.

(2) The positive criterion is *rational coherence,* the systematic interrelatedness of beliefs. Several examples can be given. First, the foregoing propositions gave an impression of coherence, for it might well rain here in October at 70° F. But the empirical scope of this set of propositions is too limited to create more than an initial credibility. For a greater degree of credibility we have to know more. For instance:

(5) I got wet on my way home.

(6) The chrysanthemums and late-blooming roses are still flourishing.

(7) I'm perspiring after running through the rain.

By enlarging the system of factual beliefs we exhibit more fully their interrelatedness as a whole, and so their believability. A convincing play or novel is, among other things, one whose many pieces hang together coherently. A historical account is said by some writers to be plausible when one event is shown to follow another in human contexts with "dramatic inevitability." This is a coherence test of truth.

Second, I referred in the last chapter to the current theological problem of relating a unique event like Christ's resurrection to the explanation given that event in Scripture. However do we get from "Jesus rose from the dead" to the explanation that "God raised him for our justification"? The explanation is twofold: causal, in that the resurrection is achieved by a God who acts in history; purposive, in that it relates to our redemption. On the one hand, no direct logical inference establishes the truth of this explanation, and on the other hand no logical inconsistency establishes its falsity.

How then do we justify believing it? The answer lies in its rational coherence with the overall Biblical account of God and his redemptive action throughout history, culminating in the claims that are made concerning the deity of the historical Jesus and the redemptive purpose of his advent and death. This was how Jesus explained things to the disciples on the Emmaus Road (Luke 24:13–27). God acts in history. He is acting for our redemption. The sufferings of the Messiah are part of that drama. The Biblical explanation of his resurrection, then, follows both as a rationally coherent part of that conceptual scheme and as a crucial ingredient in its completion.

By contrast a "wild idea" that stands all by itself, unrelated to any substantial body of knowledge, has no logical relations to recommend it. It is a maverick, a shot-in-the-dark, and we have no positive way of knowing whether it is on target. "Wild ideas" are naturally suspect. No matter how ardently I affirm that the earth rests on the backs of elephants or that murder is morally defensible, these beliefs are so devoid of logical relationship with the rest of what you know I believe that you will think me either a clown or an ignoramus or else morally perverse or crazy. You will not take such "wild" assertions seriously.

We have used examples of coherent factual beliefs and interpretive schemes. Scientists and philosophers often systematize their beliefs in deductive order because a formal logical system is the clearest sort of rational coherence available. The logical character of the whole attests the truth of the premises and of each part. But factual and formal interrelationships are not the only kinds of rational coherence and unity. World-views unify our understanding of things by introducing as a focal point of reference some particular religious or quasi-religious belief. The belief that God is creator of all, for instance, does not serve as a premise from which everything else is deducible. But it provides the unifying perspective in a Biblical view of things, and the interrelated unity of the whole attests the truth of this central belief.

Difficulties arise when a number of alternative world-views appear to provide equally unified schemes. A critical examination of the alternatives is then called for. Upon examination, some might appear to involve "wild" beliefs of an empirically inadequate or logically unrelated sort, so that the alternatives boil down to relatively few. In his *Maker of Heaven and Earth,* for instance, Langdon Gilkey sees the principal alternatives to Christian theism in patristic times as either pantheism, as in neo-Platonism, or the eternal dualism of Plato and some forms of Gnosticism. He accordingly presents the conception of a personal creator in contrast with these other options, and appraises their respective strengths and weaknesses in handling logically related questions about the intelligibility of nature, the meaning of life, the problem of evil, and our own temporality. Christian theism appears in comparison to be the most coherent option as well as the most humanly satisfying.

In more recent times, the alternative world-views appear differently, and Christianity might be set in contrast with various kinds of philosophical naturalism and idealism. In *The Nature and Destiny of Man,* for example, Reinhold Niebuhr examines naturalist and idealist perspectives on man and shows by critical comparison the greater coherence of his own formulation of a Christian view as well as its greater realism about the human condition.

In chapter four we explained how a world-view is variously elaborated in the history of philosophy with different methods and models. The inadequacies of one formulation of naturalism or idealism or Christian theism do not of themselves invalidate that perspective. They simply indicate that a particular formulation is problematic and needs improvement or change, so that one might turn to alternative formulations of the same world-view instead of abandoning it altogether. This is important in Christian apologetics, for it explains how naturalists can continue to be optimistic about such a view when one naturalistic philosophy after another (Lucretius and Hobbes, for example) has been roundly criticized, and how Christianity can survive the purported demise of its Platonic, Aristotelian, Enlightenment, and Romanticist formulations. The Christian apologist must be careful neither to overstate the force of his criticisms of other positions nor to overrate his opponents' critique of a Christian position; for both he and they might well be able to avoid the problems with which they are confronted by reformulating the underlying world-view in some new fashion. It is unfortunate that the case for Christianity is sometimes tied in people's thinking to a

Greek metaphysic, or to a Cartesian view of mind and body, or to an empiricist view of verifiability.[3]

Rational coherence, then, calls for the logical scrutiny of our beliefs. Disagreements are arguable, perhaps not to the point that they are resolved, but at least to the point that we can decide whether or not a set of beliefs seems consistent and coherent. What scope and fit and public evidence are to empirical adequacy, this kind of logical scrutiny is to rational coherence. It points up another element of universality that justifies belief. In addition to (a) the principles of induction and of non-contradiction, and (b) universal aspects of experience in a common world, and (c) public evidence, we can also appeal to (d) the logical unity of our beliefs as a whole.

## 2. Beliefs and values

Man is a valuing being as well as a thinking being who seeks empirical and rational justifications. Our values influence us in what we are prepared to believe, indeed valuing is part of believing, for believing is not a detached state of mind but a personal involvement. The wife of a soldier missing in action may be told that there is little hope of her husband returning, and may know all the reasons for that judgment, but she still cannot bring herself to believe he is dead. We may say her emotions get in the way, but there is more to it than that: she so values his return and all it stands for, that she introduces reasons why he may yet be alive. Until her values change to let her conclude otherwise, or until the evidence is utterly overwhelming, she can hardly believe he is dead.

The same is the case with religious belief. As Jesus put it (John 7:17), "if any man's will is to do [God's] will, he shall know whether the teaching is from God. . . ." Prerequisite to confident belief is a valuation of the truth that inclines the will in that direction. It is possible for a person to withhold belief because he values his present self-indulgence more than he values the truth

---

3. It is possible that alternative models and perspectives share the same or similar philosophical categories, and that there are universal category areas in addition to universal laws of logic. This is suggested by structural linguistics and anthropology, and by some philosophers. If the thesis can be elaborated, it provides a further point of universal reference in justifying beliefs.

about Jesus Christ. Prerequisite to his conversion will be a trans-
formation of his personal values: this is involved in what the
Bible calls "repentance."

But what has all this to do with the justification of belief? If our
values are cognitive as well as emotive,[4] then they should be
rationally coherent both within themselves and with our other
beliefs. Consider a case where earlier beliefs shape the values that
influence added beliefs: here the values provide a logical link
between the two sets of beliefs. For instance, because I believe
that God is creator of all, I value this world despite its thwarted
potential; this valuation in turn encourages me to believe that God
would really incarnate himself in it. Then, because I believe both
these doctrines, creation and incarnation, I see that the creative
and constructive potentials of creation and of human culture can
be redeemed. I therefore value human culture and, valuing it, I
more readily believe what the Biblical prophets say about a kingdom of God that fully realizes these positive potentials here on
earth. The overall rational coherence of such beliefs and values
attests their truth.

Two objections arise. First, granted that human values are not
purely emotive, are they not still relative? How can relative values legitimately point to universally true beliefs?

Obviously some human values are relative, the value of
money and of economic security, for example. Cultural and individual differences do exist in such regards. Some human values
may well be universal, like the value of life and liberty and
justice. Moreover, values have cognitive content, such that we
argue our value judgments and debate alternative value systems.
It is then possible to bring argument and evidence to bear in ways
that help us transcend purely individual and cultural considerations and move towards the universal. As in debates about facts
and their meaning and about world-views, so it is in debates
about values; similar procedures and criteria operate. Our values
must stand up before (a) universal laws of logic, (b) universal

---

4. The emotivist theory of value proposed by the positivists has been rightly
   criticized for failing to see that we argue our value judgments. Values relate
   to thought as well as feeling; they are conceptions of the good, ideals that we
   seek, shaped reflectively in the light of our present needs and future possibilities as well as by what else we believe. See C.S. Lewis, *The Abolition
   of Man* (Macmillan, 1947) and G.J. Warnock, *Contemporary Moral Philosophy* (Macmillan, 1967), chapter three.

aspects of experience, (c) public evidence, and (d) the logical unity of our beliefs.

The actual values we hold, moreover, have to do with what I shall call (e) *universal value-areas*. All men in all cultures and at all points in history hold values in the area of physical life and well-being; the particular formulations may vary, producing disagreements about abortion, euthanasia, capital punishment, war, restrictions on the possession of lethal weapons, and so forth, but we all make value judgments of some sort in this general area. Likewise in the area of sex and marriage: particular formulations may allow monogamy, polygamy, or concubinage, even homosexual behavior and group marriages, but we all develop values in this area. So too with economic values: anthropologists find that the formulated rights and rules about work and property vary, but values are nonetheless evident in regard to a man's work or property or to those of his family or tribe.

Within each area a particular morality formulates its beliefs. Christians (and others) argue for some universally binding general rule in each area, such as those we find in the second half of the decalog. We are likely to disagree about their application, for instance to capital punishment or war. We may regard these as legitimate but tragic exceptions to the rule about killing, or we may argue that they too are wrong. But the point is, first, that we argue our differences and so bring them to some degree under logical and factual control and, second, that value-areas are universal even if the particular formulations are not. For these two reasons the values that help shape beliefs are not entirely relative. Insofar as we can show that our value judgments are rationally coherent and universally applicable, to that extent a resultant belief is not entirely relative to the individual or his culture but lays claim to universal truth.

The second objection also is an old one. If our values influence our beliefs and if we value intellectual honesty, then should not honesty keep us from believing anything unless we are certain? William K. Clifford argued in his well-known essay, "The Ethics of Belief," that it is always wrong to stifle doubt and to believe something on insufficient evidence. Certainly the Christian should value intellectual honesty and should not want to stifle serious doubt. The question is rather about what constitutes *sufficient* evidence. When is the empirical evidence *adequate?* What *degree* of coherence is sufficient to justify belief?

Two initial observations should help. First, what is sufficient to justify belief may not be sufficient to resolve all the theoretical problems, eliminate all the other options, or allay every possible doubt. And the degree of evidence that is sufficient to justify a relatively trivial belief—trivial because so few values are at stake (e.g., "this cake looks fresher than that one")—may not be sufficient in regard to a more momentous one (e.g., "capital punishment deters criminals").

Second, we frequently face a conflict of values in regard to belief as we do in other decisions. The value of intellectual caution and reserved judgment sometimes conflicts with other equally important values that are at stake in a particular belief. If my house is on fire and my life is at stake, I will risk acting on the tenuous belief that I could survive a jump from the second floor. Yet I would be a fool to jump just to prove the point. The justification of belief is related to the values at stake.

William James' response to Clifford was not unlike this. In his famous essay "The Will to Believe," he points out that options may be living or dead, forced or avoidable, momentous or trivial. A genuine option is one that is living, forced, and momentous. Decision cannot always be avoided, but if it cannot be made on purely intellectual grounds then our "passional nature" must decide in terms of the biological and psychological consequences of belief.

James' pragmatism does not satisfy me, for he assumes an intellect-emotion dichotomy which I have attempted to avoid. If thought and emotion unite in our valuing, then what James calls a genuine option is one that involves not so much a conflict between reason and emotion as a conflict of values. In complex moral and political decisions, we learn to resolve value conflicts either in favor of higher values (choosing the lesser of two evils), or in favor of the alternative that coheres more fully with all the evidence and all else we believe. There is nothing dishonest about this. It is rather the kind of unavoidable decision which human life with its complexities and perversions throws at us repeatedly.

Underlying both this response to Clifford's objection and the overall attempt to incorporate the role of values into the justification of belief, is the view of man which we previously introduced. Clifford seems to suppose that the ideal man is Descartes' rational being who withholds all judgment and action until he can be ruled by objective reason alone, so that values other than the value of rational objectivity and honesty are irrelevant to belief. But if other values too have been subjected to significant argument and realignment, they are not irrelevant to the justification of belief. And if man is not a purely rational being but also a valuing being, then the values he has carefully scrutinized may legitimately be considered in the appraisal of a belief. A man ideally acts and believes as a whole person: a rational and a valuing being and a purposeful agent who acts.

## 3. Beliefs and action

A man not only thinks and values, he also has projects in which he acts. His thinking and valuing shape his projects, determine the means he adopts, and thereby guide his actions. Reciprocally his projects shape his thinking and influence his beliefs. This aspect of our being has been stressed by both pragmatists and existentialists. John Dewey argues that thought is always directed towards the resolution of practical problems and that the beliefs we hold are relative to the particular problem situations they address. There is no universal and unchanging truth to be believed. Sartre meantime speaks of everything a man says and does and of his whole life as a project related to the very meaning of his existence. Words and deeds and beliefs and actions are his attempts to make a place for himself in an otherwise empty and alien world, for again there is no universally true and unchanging meaning in life. While I am not satisfied with these analyses of human action, they do emphasize the primacy of the practical and uncover the influence of action-projects on our beliefs.

But essentially the same question arises as in the relation of values to beliefs: are beliefs always relative to different action-projects? My response is essentially the same as before: insofar as in our projects we debate our goals and reason about the application of means to ends, to that extent our projects and the beliefs they engender are exposed to rational controls. Only if our projects are capriciously selected and if our means are utterly random, only then will the beliefs involved seem utterly relative. That beliefs relate to purposes and projects, therefore, means that they address a definable problem, not that they are devoid of reasonableness or of any relevance to others.

This initial sketch will become more concrete as we consider two specific forms of the "relativity" objection.[5] The first comes from people like Feuerbach and Freud who see a belief as a psychological projection of needs or wishes we are struggling to fulfil. Belief in God is the extension of infantile dependence on a parent figure, perhaps of an Oedipus complex. Marx saw religion as the "opiate of the masses," a sublimation of revolutionary energies through wishful religious and utopian thinking. Others regard metaphysical beliefs as rationalizations of suppressed wishes for a more ideal world. In any case beliefs are supposedly relative to variable psychological conditions, and are thereby detached from the universality of truth which we seek.

We cannot deny that under pathological conditions people create imaginary worlds in which to live, and that fiction writers and ordinary people like to imagine. But Freud and the others build theories of normal behavior on abnormal cases in which fiction is truth and truth fiction, a procedure which has been criticized by psychologists and philosophers of science. We are more concerned to uncover universal conditions of belief in normal behavior. From a logical point of view, the claim that antecedent psychological or economic conditions are a sufficient cause for belief commits the fallacy of *post hoc ergo propter hoc* ("after this, therefore on account of this"). Psychological conditions of some sort may be necessary to belief, but that is not to say they are a sufficient condition. Empirical and logical conditions must be added if we are to give a sufficient account. It is the universal elements in belief and action that afford checks on the relativity of belief.

Freud's belief about human beliefs can be no exception to his rule: if all human beliefs are simply projections of our psychological needs and relative thereto, so too are his beliefs. Neither Freud nor Marx nor any other such critic can consistently claim universal truth for his own position. And what would end rational dialog in the dark night of depth psychology or the rhetoric and violence of the class struggle. The only resolution would be pragmatic: the survival of the fittest in which might makes right. Such a *reductio ad absurdum* is no resolution at all, but forces us to other ways of justifying truth claims.

---

5. Yet another form, the relativity of beliefs to sociological factors, is discussed by Roger Trigg in *Reason and Commitment* (Cambridge, 1973).

This response to the relativity objection suggests another form of the same objection. We have agreed with John Dewey that the practical problems confronting us influence our beliefs, but Dewey took it further than this. In the evolutionary process governed by natural selection, problems and projects change and our beliefs have to vary accordingly. Although we accumulate a wealth of "funded experience" on which to draw as need arises, as long as situations and problems change there can be no unchanging and universal truth. All beliefs have purely temporary application and are subject to change in the course of time.

Our first response is that this conclusion rests on precarious presuppositions. Whatever one thinks of the theory of natural selection as a biological explanation, Dewey has extended it to embrace all human thought and action. This "universalization" of a theory initially addressed to a limited area of investigation pushes it out of science and into metaphysics. Dewey is thus an evolutionary naturalist: that is, he sees man entirely as a part and product of nature, and explains nature entirely in terms of mechanisms at work uniformly from its lowest to its highest levels, the mechanisms of natural selection. These presuppositions lead him to view ideas and beliefs as nothing but workable solutions to changing problems, and so to regard all truth as relative. The evolutionary model combines with his naturalistic perspective to produce this result.

Now although I agree that belief is action-related and project-dependent, as a Christian I am not a philosophical naturalist like Dewey and I do not interpret man and his actions entirely in terms of natural selection. God's creation is not without universal structures, and man in God's creation is not in such flux as to lack all universal points of reference. His projects arise within the ordered creation of God. If we can identify (f) *universal action-projects* to which man addresses his beliefs, then the truth of those beliefs is not as relative as Dewey supposes.

Let me reiterate what marks off the theist's view from Dewey's: our projects arise within the ordered creation of God. Man and the world in which he must act are not the chance product of a blind evolutionary process, but the purposively ordered outcome of divine creation, somewhat distorted now to be sure, but still attesting the wisdom and purpose of God. Christian writers therefore speak of "orders of creation" or of "law spheres." Our economic activity, family activity, political activity, and so forth, each takes its place within environmental structures and in relation to structures of personality that God creatively ordained. In all his actions man relates not to a world of evolutionary uncertainties that may as easily destroy as preserve him, but to an ordered creation of which he is an intended part. Man's task is to find his place and exercise his role in each area of his life in accordance with its natural order ordained by God.

This first response to Dewey exposes his naturalistic premise and offers theistic premises as an alternative way of viewing the relation of belief to actions. Our second response now points to universal human projects. For Dewey, thought addresses itself on an *ad hoc* basis to particular technological, political, economic, and social problems that emerge and require resolution. But if each such area of activity is ultimately ordered neither by chance processes nor by man's adjustment skills but by God, then what a man comes in the process to believe should be governed by what he finds is universal about that order of creation, not just by the *ad hoc* demands of an immediate problem. His beliefs need not be entirely relative, but can accumulate as an interrelated whole—as is the world we inhabit and as is truth itself.

Dewey's analogue to this is "funded experience": but funded experience is an accumulation of "how-to-do-its" that may or may not have future application, not a growing approximation to universal truth about the essential order of creation.

When, for example, I am faced with alternative political beliefs, I cannot decide how to act or vote in a particular situation on purely pragmatic grounds. Rather, I must justify my beliefs, be they politically conservative or liberal, in relation to my understanding of political morality, the essential nature of human society, and the place of the political order in God's creation. This involves consideration of Biblical materials on the role of the civil authorities in maintaining peace and furthering justice in a world twisted by sin, a grasp of the moral as well as the political dimension of the present situation, and an understanding of the political philosophies which guide our present governmental policies and actions. A particular political belief is justified by its coherence within my total understanding of the political order as it applies to the problem at hand. This too is a rational test.

The relation of a belief to a particular problem does not then deprive that belief of universal controls, because the universal orders of creation within which particular problems arise are subject to the law and purposes of God, and the belief in question is justified by its coherence within our larger understanding of appropriate creation orders.

But in addition to having political and other universal projects, man believes and acts in relation to the overall project of his life. What is life as a whole about? What is its purpose? A world-view is a belief about life as a whole; it concerns the overall project of human existence in which I participate. Are world-views entirely relative?

Again the response is that relativism fails, for the overall project of human existence,, like each man's life and each particular area of life, has universal dimensions. A world-view attempts to respond to a universal question about the meaning of human existence. Any question demands an answer addressed to the question in mind. Not any response will do, but only one which in fact speaks to the question. A question implies a job description which its answer must fit; it implies criteria applicable to any and every answer to it anyone ever proposes, criteria which in that sense are universal.

What are the criteria implicit in the world-view question? Can we elicit them? I think so.

First, the demand for a *unifying* world-view by which to live (i.e., the overall project of human life) asks for an understanding that sees all the various areas of life as an interrelated whole, one that helps us keep the parts in meaningful relation to the whole. This is *rational coherence*.

Second, the demand is for a unifying *world*-view, one that embraces all aspects of experience without squeezing them into unrealistic shapes, one that is true to both frustrating and fulfilling experiences. This is *empirical adequacy*.

Third, the demand is for a unifying world-view with which we can *live* meaningfully and which can guide both thought and action. This demand for meaning-giving power suggests a more fully personal test of relevance to universal value-areas and universal action-projects (or orders of creation). We may call it *human relevance* to stress the subjective or personal side of truth as compared with an objectively intellectual consideration of facts and arguments. "Personal relevance" might serve as long as we take "personal" to mean the universally human rather than what is basically individualistic, for the demands of my individual idiosyncrasies are relative to those idiosyncrasies and say nothing about the possible universal truth of my beliefs.

These three tests reflect both the nature of the world-view question and the generic nature of the man who asks the question. They satisfy his universal demands as a rational being, valuing being, and personal agent. One of the criteria may apply more than others to the truth of a particular proposition, so that a more purely empirical belief is more readily justified by its empirical adequacy, but all these tests are applicable at times and all of them together apply to world-views. They are not utterly conclusive in their decisions. They do not end argument or unbelief. But they bear witness to the universality of truth; they justify believing we have transcended the purely individual and relative because now we judge what we believe by what is universal. We are finite: whatever our tests of truth, we still know in part and see through a glass darkly.

In summary, we can judge a belief in the light of:

(a) universal laws of logic,

(b) universal aspects of human experience,

(c) public evidence,

(d) the logical unity of a set of beliefs,

(e) universal value areas,

and (f) universal action-projects in the various orders of creation.

## 4. The witness of the Holy Spirit

Theologians speak of the witness of the Holy Spirit. How does this pertain to what we have been saying? The particular Biblical passages involved (John 14:26; 15:26; 16:7-15) do not refer to the truth of our scientific, political, or philosophical beliefs. Rather they teach that the Holy Spirit bears witness to Jesus Christ and guides us to the truth of the gospel, by reminding us of Jesus' teaching about sin, righteousness, and judgment and by convicting us of our need for his grace. Translated into the terms of our discussion, it means that God helps us see the *personal relevance* of the Christian message to our overall life-project, and this produces changes in both our beliefs and our values.

While the pertinent Biblical passages do not speak directly to other matters, two observations seem to follow. First, inasmuch as the truth about Jesus Christ and his gospel has implications that reach beyond what the Bible explicitly teaches, the witness of the Holy Spirit is pertinent to our thinking even where Scripture is silent. Yet this does not bypass rational considerations or other justifications of what we believe, for the Holy Spirit attests truth in relation to Jesus Christ, in and through our consideration of the discernible implications of the Christian faith for human thought and action in one area or another. The Christian revelation is after all cognitive as well as personal, both in its divine source and its human impact.

Second, the witness of the Holy Spirit is not a mystical experience unrelated to Biblical exegesis or to the human imagination or to scientific inquiry or philosophical analysis. His is rather a mind-clearing and thought-focussing activity that illumines the understanding and helps us get things in clearer relationship to the essential content of the Christian faith. We grasp more plainly what the Scriptures teach, we make it more fully our own, and we recognize how other things relate rationally to Christian belief. The Christian indeed asks God's guidance in intellectual tasks, but the Holy Spirit is neither a short-cut to knowledge nor the producer of some infallible human understanding that would make us something other than the fallible but growing human beings God created us to be.

What difference exists, then, between the Christian thinker aided by the Holy Spirit and any other thinker? The difference is not that the one has private sources of information that are closed to the other, nor that he becomes a better thinker than the other, nor that when they disagree he is always right. The difference is rather that his final rule of faith and practice is clearly identified as the Scriptures, and the focus of his thinking will be the focal point in the ultimate unity of truth: Jesus Christ as creator and lord.

# EIGHT

# Christ the Truth

Jesus Christ called himself the Truth. In the immediate context, the emphasis may well be on his personal fidelity: we can trust him to bring us to the Father. But in the larger Biblical context more is implied. He is himself the eternal God, the ultimate source of all truth and of our capacity for knowing anything at all. All the treasures of wisdom and knowledge come into focus in a unified world-and-life view in relation to himself, the creator-God. The Christian is often reminded that how he treats his neighbor, how he regards his natural environment, and how he cares for his own body all reflect his attitude to the God of creation. By the same token, how he regards learning and how he concerns himself with the pursuit of truth, regardless of his field of inquiry, reflect his attitude to Christ the Truth.

The Christian of all people, we have observed, has good reasons for believing in truth. He has good reasons for believing it to be universal and unchanging, and good reasons for being concerned about the unifying truth of a Biblical world-view. He has good reasons also for emphasizing sound logic, for testing what he hears by rational means. And he has good reasons for doing this in whatever field he is engaged. For all truth is God's truth, and the believer is called to attest it by both his life and his thought. His relationship to Jesus Christ creates concern about truth.

## 1. Motivation

Christ the Truth becomes the dominant motivation in intellectual inquiry. No dichotomy of sacred and secular tasks can be allowed, and no subject is exempt. The student will therefore welcome truth and submit to it wherever it is found, out of obedience to Christ. Academic work becomes an opportunity to extend the Lordship of Christ over the mind; thought merges into worship.

## 2. World-view

Since Christ the Truth is the unifying focus of the Biblical world-view, to think "Christianly" is to think "world-viewishly." This means we locate each field of inquiry within a Christian understanding of life as a whole, and that we interpret what we know in that larger context. The key ingredients of such a world-view will include the Biblical conceptions of nature, of man, and of history, in relation to the God we know in Christ. To think "Christianly" is to bring these concepts into our thinking about everything else.[1] This, in fact, is what I have tried to do in thinking about truth and knowledge.

The Biblical view of nature stands in contrast to Greek ideas. There man dares to wrestle secrets from the world, his mind and will challenging fate. In the Bible, nature reveals its ways to the wondering mind, and man worships God for what he sees. For the Greeks, matter is chaotic, the cause of evil; the body handicaps the mind, and its passions allure the will. But in the Bible, material things bear witness to the greatness of God who declared what he had made to be "good." It is not the body that makes a man sin—in fact, the resurrection of the body is a cardinal Christian belief; it is from the heart that sin proceeds, from its criminal negligence about God, and from the idolatrous and evil desires that result.

The significance of this view of nature pervades theology and reaches into every other area of inquiry. The value of all creation is reaffirmed by God's continued involvement in it. He does not leave it to its fate. The incarnation of Jesus Christ shouts to all men that nature is not itself evil but good. Evil is not intrinsic to nature, but is rather a corruption of the good. Yet the good will be restored. By God's grace all things will be made new.

That nature is good gives meaning to life. It means that ours is not a world of unrelated events without rhyme or reason or pur-

---

1. For a fuller account, see the article on "Christian Philosophy" in *Encyclopedia Britannica*, 15th edition.

pose. Fact and value are tied together in the very nature of creation, and nature will by the goodness of God fulfil the purposes for which it was created. This hope focusses in Jesus Christ, the meaning-giving *Logos* by whom and for whom all things exist.

It is here that the Christian rests his confidence that rational and scientific inquiry can bring good results, that the technology we develop can either bless us or curse us, according to the wisdom and morality with which we use it. Here too rests the Christian artist's belief that he can take matter and shape a thing of beauty, for man was made by God, a created creator, to create things that God himself only made possible. Art can ennoble the heart of man and enrich his life, or it can prostitute him, according to the wisdom which the aesthetic life, like the scientific, enfolds. Here also rests the confidence that nature's resources are available for men to respect, not to abuse, and that men and women can be educated to understand and to benefit from the world that God has made. To think Christianly, we must locate our arts and sciences, our educational and our social tasks, within this Christian view of nature.

The Biblical view of man, likewise, differs from both Greek and modern ideas. Man is made of the dust of the earth, part of nature, yet he is uniquely in the image of God. It is not enough, then, to think of man as taming nature or ruling it by reason alone. For as part of nature man is ruled rather than the ruler; and as a creature he is servant rather than lord. Yet he is created in God's image to fulfil a high calling. He is God's viceroy, mandated to preserve, develop, and employ the resources of nature for the glory of their maker. He is also a societal being, made to pursue his calling in community with others and in communion with God. Not only art and science can be God's calling to me, therefore, but also family life, political life, business and social enterprises, and the affairs of the church. We must see our sciences and our humanities in this light. Man's sin against God and his inhumanity to other men do not put a halt to this calling: they obscure the purpose, distort the understanding, twist the values, and pervert the performance. But in Christ God calls men back to the task. In fact, Jesus Christ as the perfect man exemplifies the ideal of one who was part of nature, for he took the form of a servant, yet who fulfilled his mandate in community with men and in communion with the Father.

This view of man challenges Enlightenment aspirations to make man's reason the ruler of all, and it challenges Romanticist dreams that absorb man wholly into nature itself—views that still find expression today. It suggests to the behavioral scientist that if there is more to man than the dust of the earth, then there is more to him than overt behavior reveals. While there is room for all that science can observe, the findings of science must be seen in the larger context.

The Biblical understanding of history is equally crucial to a Christian world-view. It follows from what we have said of nature and of man, for if nature has purpose and value as God's creation, and man is part of nature, then the history of man has purpose and value too. God gives history meaning, not just through man's achievements as today's humanists would have us think, nor just through crisis events by which he breaks into history. God does not have to break in, for he is immanent as well as transcendent; the Old Testament sees his creative hand in all that transpires.

History is the arena of God's creative and redemptive work and of man in the image of God. History is not relentlessly determined by economic or other forces, for man remains a free agent, responsible for the historical consequences of his own actions. Man, too, is a history-maker, who makes history by what he knows and what he does, by his science and his art, his economic and political actions, and by his religious involvement. The Bible, therefore, presents a moral interpretation of history, in which men and nations are held accountable. Their destiny is not shaped by an impersonal force so much as by what they are themselves and by the consequences of their deeds which God's judgment secures. Our attempts to understand and to shape history, be it political, economic, intellectual, or religious, must be seen in this light.

Yet there is hope in history. The Cross provides a paradigm case, where the sin of man is overcome by the grace of God, and evil is made to serve the good. So it will be in history's final outcome. Our hope is ultimately not in man's resourcefulness, created though he was to be creative; he creates problems as well as solving them, and his utopian dreams are bound to be frustrated. The Christian will therefore avoid both an unqualified pessimism and an unqualified optimism about the future. Historical progress is possible by virtue of both the resources of nature and the resourcefulness of men, progress in understanding, in science, and in technology, and progress thereby in resolving one problem or another that arises in government or elsewhere. But history remains a creation of God.

I have summarized the Biblical view of nature, of man, and of history because these concepts unify our thinking about everything else, and unify it in relation to Jesus Christ. All our science and our art, all our social and academic tasks have to do directly or indirectly with nature, man, and history. These concepts, therefore, define the contours of a world-view within which our particular callings take their place. They give what we do basis, purpose, and hope. They underscore our responsibility to think Christianly and to contribute to the history of those ventures in which we engage.

### 3. Emphasizing truth

That Christ is the Truth also leads us to emphasize truth in what we do. (a) We must emphasize it in *education,* both in our own schooling and in considering the teaching profession as a Christian vocation.[2]

If we believe that Christ is the Truth and that all truth is his, we will not be content with a training that merely develops vocational or professional skills rather than emphasizing the pursuit of truth itself. Schools and colleges and some universities are often geared to training rather than to education *per se,* and especially so in the developing nations. Moreover, we live in an intensely pragmatic age that wants perpetually to know about the practical uses of learning, and defines "practical" to mean "earning capacity"—a sad commentary on our truncated values and loss of truth. A student would surprise us all if he simply said he were "going into truth." Christians perpetuate the mistake: they tend to add to a student's future earning capacity nothing but the opportunities for witness afforded by his "training," or the apologetic value of his learning, or some other pragmatic function it may have. We hardly seem to believe in truth in any larger sense than that.

If we believe in Christ the Truth, we will also disclaim the

---

2. See further J. H. Newman's classic *The Idea of a University;* Arnold Nash's *The University and the Modern World* (Macmillan, 1944); and this author's *The Idea of a Christian College* (Eerdmans, 1975).

notion that education is simply learning more and more disjointed information or, as some wag has put it, learning more and more about less and less. Some degree of specialization is of course necessary, but not without and not before one has learned to see things whole. Specialization unrelated to the larger concerns of men and society can become a technological monster that dehumanizes people rather than making them more "truly" human, as education should. Fragmented information produces connoisseurs at best and a tragic confusion of thought and action at worst. But if all truth is ultimately one coherent whole, then an education that is concerned with the truth will impart a vision of the whole and some understanding of how within that whole my particular field depends on and contributes to its neighbors. The Christian especially will seek this in his own learning and will want to impart it to others through his own teaching.

I am not suggesting that truth is the only concern of education. Further aims can readily be elicited from the account we gave in the previous chapter of the nature of persons. If man is a rational being, we must indeed cultivate the mind, inform the understanding, and teach him to think for himself and communicate with clarity and cogency. If man is also a valuing being, education must engage his thinking about values—moral and social values, aesthetic and religious values—and must teach him to make defensible value judgments and help him launch their implementation. If man is a historical agent, one who must act responsibly in society, participating in and shaping his own and others' history, then education must teach responsible decision making and prepare a person for effective social action and cultural activity that ranges far beyond the way he earns a living to the totality of his engagement in life.

But contemporary education seems concerned with vocational skills, personality development, interpersonal relations, and unstructured "learning experiences" at the expense of truth. If man is to be man and to live life whole in God's world, then the loss of truth in education must be reversed. The Christian should be the first to see this and to act accordingly. Whatever the other proper concerns of education, truth—wherever it be found—is a *sine qua non.*

Contemporary education suffers from all three aspects of the loss of truth we noted in chapter one: a loss of focus on truth, a loss of the universality of truth, and a loss of the unity of truth.

Christians stand in a remarkably strategic position to help education retrieve this loss, for we of all people believe in truth and
want to keep it in focus. In our pluralistic society, moreover,
where truth often appears relative rather than universal, Christianity has a historical role that enables it to articulate the theistic
basis that makes truth universally the same. And in this age of
fragmented specialization that easily despairs of finding any unifying meaning to life and thought, the Christian endeavors to see
all truth everywhere in relation to the God revealed in Jesus
Christ. To apply this to all we know is a mammoth task, but if as
a Christian I sincerely believe in truth, then I cannot avoid my
part of the responsibility.

A thorough Biblical understanding is mandatory. By and large,
the kind of Bible teaching imparted in church and Sunday School,
guided as it is by primarily evangelistic, pastoral, and devotional
aims, is starkly inadequate. The average church member without
other input into his thinking may know Bible characters and some
outlines of Bible history, he may be acquainted with the miracles
and parables of Jesus and the moral teachings of the New Testament, and be able to discuss the doctrine of salvation and how the
churches differ in their ordinances and organization, but his grasp
of Biblical theology, systematically developed in application to
the life and thought either of Biblical times or his own culture, is
sadly lacking.

It is not enough to include Biblical and religious studies in the
curriculum. They are important, for modern man remains unedu-
cated without some knowledge of his religious heritage. And how
can he think Christianly without a thorough knowledge of the
Bible? But Biblical and religious studies of themselves do not
retrieve the loss of truth in education, for at least two reasons.
First, relativism has intruded into religion too, so that the Bible's
teaching is too often viewed as culturally relative and in need of
change. This was the tenor of liberal theology and it persists in
the existential hermeneutic of today. Second, religious studies
often become compartmentalized like any other discipline, instead of intruding their unifying vision into other areas of study.
Unfortunately, one can study religion and the Bible without learning to think Christianly about science and art and human society.

The crucial question for the recovery of truth, however, is how
a Christian world-view can be introduced into education. My
point is not that it ought not be excluded but that in practice,

when we think Christianly, it cannot possibly be left out. Our world-view shows itself in the way we shape and relate our ideas and see everything in relation to God.

The Christian teacher cannot hide the truth. He would be dishonest if he denied that his world-view affected his thinking and his teaching. Intellectual honesty consists not in forcing an impossible neutrality, but in admitting that neutrality is not possible. It consists in confessing and scrutinizing one's point of view and the difference that it makes, and in explaining how other points of view would have to disagree. Nor need the teacher suppose that this is unprofessional or unethical: it is no more a matter of preaching or proselytizing for the Christian than for anyone else, despite the influence on others' beliefs, for everyone has some view of life that comes through in how he thinks and acts and what he says.

If I believe in truth, I will then regard my own education as a glorious opportunity to explore truth wherever it is found, and to uncover its theistic foundations, and to see the bearing of my theology on what I learn. I will accept the challenge of interpreting things aright, and will embrace every field of endeavor within the meaning-giving compass of my faith. If I believe in truth, I will also see that education is a strategic professional field for obeying the cultural mandate, for where can Christian thinking have more far-reaching influence towards overcoming the loss of truth?

In thinking Christianly about our various fields it is often best to start by thinking historically. Other things must follow, such as philosophy of science, philosophy of history, political and ethical theory, aesthetics, and so forth, but the history of Christianity and culture is an essential start. The reason for this is that Christians comprise a historical community. The evangelical with his "minority complex" often forgets that he is part of a massive historical movement much larger than his own kind of church. Catholic and Protestant thought of various sorts, and Eastern Orthodoxy, can all be of help, for they share with him the basics of Biblical theism. The evangelical tends to see himself today standing alone, he supposes that nobody ever faced such issues as he now faces, and he therefore thinks in a vacuum. But he is part of a community that also is part of a historical community that has wrestled with intellectual and social and cultural issues many times.

Four things emerge from an historical approach. First, Christian attitudes to culture have varied from uncritical acceptance to an overly critical rejection of almost everything. We spoke of this earlier, and the reader can explore such attitudes further in Richard Niebuhr's *Christ and Culture*. Second, Christians have contributed immensely to every academic field: they have contributed a motivation born of confidence in the goodness and intelligence of the creator, and they have contributed insight concerning the intelligibility of nature and the value of man. But they also worked some of the implications of these insights into the details of their fields. We must not forget that medievals like Augustine and Aquinas, and moderns like Newton, Descartes, Leibniz, and Locke were themselves earnest and scholarly Christians. And writers like T. S. Eliot, François Mauriac, and Flannery O'Connor give literary expression to a Christian view of man. Their work is at our disposal. Third, second-hand benefits accrue through the influence of Christianity on those who were not themselves practicing believers. Kant, for instance, retained the influence of his early pietist training in the value he placed on morality and human freedom; and existentialism, for all its nihilistic excesses, originated in some of its proponents as an attempt to preserve human freedom and meaningful individuality, a Christian inheritance progressively lost during the eighteenth and nineteenth centuries. Fourth, Christian self-understanding has gained from its own history of intellectual involvement. The history of theology was much enriched by interaction with philosophy and science, enriched in its methods, in the elaboration of its doctrine, and in understanding its own relevance to human life and thought.

(b) If we believe that Christ is the truth we will also emphasize *truth in the arts*. What about literature and painting and sculpture and music and drama? Some Christian groups give them even less attention than other cultural activities as if art, being non-utilitarian, is frivolous or irrelevant to the weightier matters of law and grace. Do the arts really merit serious Christian involvement? Do we have as clear a mandate here as in more theoretical fields?

Various reasons might of course be given in support of an affirmative answer. But in addition to the fact that man is by his very nature a creative and artistic being, in addition to the values of beauty and creativity, and to the social functions of the arts, they also have truth-value.

Some disclaimers are needed. First, in speaking of truth in art I am not referring just to explicitly religious art that tells of God or the gospel. There is a great amount of superb work of this sort, of course, ranging from the cathedral at Chartres to the cathedral at Coventry, from Michelangelo and Rembrandt to Bach and Handel, from the Old Testament psalms to contemporary hymns. But just as truth itself is larger than explicitly religious truths, for all truth about everything is indeed God's, so truth in art is considerably more widespread than in religious art *per se*. And just as art itself has more functions than the directly religious one of assisting worship and meditation, so the range of truth in art itself is more varied. In fact, while medieval art noticeably concentrated on religious themes and strained to move beyond the present world, post-Reformation painters felt free to delight in the physical world around them and to look more closely at the face of man. Religious renewal enriches our appreciation of earth and of all things great and small that God has made.

Second, we must not superimpose on art a correspondence theory of truth that expects a straightforward agreement between artistic representation and the world it is about. Truth in art does not require an objective, point-by-point copy of reality. Even photography as an art is not that slavish. The artist is a created creator who imagines new worlds, shapes fresh experiences, and reinterprets the old. If we take truth to require slavish copying, then Pablo Picasso is right when he says that art is a lie. But his fuller statement is more to the point: ''Art is a lie that makes us realize truth, at least the truth that is given us to understand.''[3]

The notion that art copies reality seems to come from the Greeks. Plato developed it in his *Republic,* and rated the various arts according to their closeness to the eternal forms. But that presupposes that all reality is preformed, fixed by the rational necessity of the forms rather than open to new creative possibilities, and it assumes that man at his best will copy what is given rather than creating for himself. Plato's world is in this

---

3. Quoted in *Christian Faith and the Contemporary Arts,* ed. Finley Ebersole (Abingdon Press, 1957), p. 6.

regard an impersonal sort of place inhabited by less than fully personal men.

The fallacy that art is a true copy of reality underlies the demand that it be didactic. Art can of course teach, but it is not valued primarily, if at all, for its didactic qualities. Indeed, the artist is likely to complain that didacticism prostitutes art and robs it of its integrity. We must not expect to find truth as forthrightly stated in art as in a scientific essay, a Biblical exposition, or an ethical treatise.

Third, we must avoid another Platonic mistake that equates truth with beauty. This equation too was made possible by the view that fixed and eternal forms provide both patterns for physical particulars (hence truth) and harmoniously ordered unities for aesthetic contemplation (hence beauty). To intuit truth and to contemplate beauty, therefore, amount to essentially the same thing. Attention here is focussed on the form rather than the content of a work of art, on how well it represents the universal rather than on how it reveals the novel and unique, on the cognitive value of art rather than its imaginative and evocative power, on man objectively conceived rather than on the human self perceived from within. It is a view of art which may in measure fit Greek music and sculpture but which, as Plato and Aristotle well knew, casts doubt on arts like literature and drama that portray particular people and their actions.

But my objection to the equation of truth and beauty is to more than the Greek theory of forms and more than its attitude to literature and drama. The Christian believes that truth is unchanging and universal and one, because he believes in a transcendent God who wisely creates an intelligently ordered world. It makes sense to ascribe truth to God. But the case of beauty is different. Denis de Rougemont claims that "beauty" is not a biblical notion or term. This may not be strictly correct, but I have to agree with him that the Scriptures do not tell us that God is Beauty. Rather they say that God is Love and that Christ is the Way, the Truth, and the Life.

> This way is not beautiful, but rough and painful. This truth is not beautiful, but liberating. This life does not open into beautiful harmonies, but passes by the narrow gate of death.[4]

---

4. *Ibid.*

We are called to worship God "in the beauty of holiness" and to "behold the beauty of the Lord," but it is not clear in those contexts whether beauty is an attribute of God or of man's experience of God. In any case, artistic beauty has to do with the senses and the imagination, with the tempo and rhythm we feel, the tone and melody and harmony we hear, the light and color and arrangement we see, the imaginative scenes we picture in our minds. But God is Spirit, an immaterial being who has neither physical senses nor sense experiences of his own, and who cannot be physically felt or seen or heard or even pictured outside of some theophany or else the Incarnation. Yet God is indeed Truth, and he knows and understands all truth about everything in creation. Truth is different from beauty.

We should think of beauty rather as created than as an attribute of God. The experience of beauty is possible because men are created with capacity for aesthetic delight in created things, and physical things are created with the power of producing that delight. All beauty and every possibility of beauty comes from God. It is one of his good gifts to men, to be received with thanksgiving. It develops in us the capacity to value our bodily existence in the world that God has made.

So much for disclaimers. Granted that there is more to art than truth and that the truth in art is neither slavish correspondence to reality nor only that of explicitly religious themes, in what ways is art true?

Artists speak of the integrity and honesty of a work of art. In a piece that has integrity, the artist is neither playing to the galleries by parading his skills nor playing a game of make-believe about life. Art is serious work that grapples with life the way it is or could be; it is not an escape. The painter must be true to his own perception of things, the playwright must let a character be himself rather than an unreal phony. Fiction must be believable, true to the way people are in their hopes and frustrations, even though the events it portrays occur only in the imagination. Even mythological and fantasy literature have integrity, for they create new worlds and new kinds of beings that must remain true to what they are. Truth in art means being faithful to a theme, to a genre, to the materials in use, to the artistic task. This is the personal side of truth.

But there is more to it than this. The fact is, I believe, that the arts can tell the truth more completely, in more depth, and more realistically than the sciences with their controlled data and theoretical abstractions often can. Consider this, that while ancient and medieval scientists hold little more than antiquarian interest for scientists today, yet we still read Homer and Sophocles and Dante, and view the Parthenon and the Sistine Chapel both for their intrinsic worth and for the lasting truth they reveal. Consider also that the various nuances of a drama combine to say more about one character than we might learn in a thousand encounters of a more objective sort. Consider too that the arts are purveyors of world-views: they help us envision a unity of truth that our scientific age has lost.

The artist speaks by creating symbols. A symbol differs from a univocal term in two regards: it reveals more of reality than it explicitly denotes, and it uncovers to us what lies within ourselves. Think of Shylock's "pound of flesh" and the thoughts of vengeful cruelty it still evokes. Think of Lady Macbeth's inerasable spot and how dramatically it uncovers our own sin and guilt. Think how Wordsworth's daffodils convey a Romantic vision of life. Recall the symbolism in church architecture and clerical vestments. Think of the revealing symbols in Biblical literature: God is both king and fortress, Christ is both shepherd and sacrificial lamb, the church is both his body and his bride. The ordinances of the church are loaded with symbolic significance; in fact, some theologians see that as their primary value.

But what of contemporary literature and art? Here too truth will out. Tennessee Williams' *A Streetcar Named Desire* exposes not just a tawdry world in New Orleans, not only the seamy circumstances and emotions of the characters it portrays, but it more ultimately helps us look with honesty at the human condition, fraught as it is by the inescapable dilemmas our passions unavoidably create. We see ourselves mirrored in the tragic self-deceptions of a fallen woman who is both loved and despised, and we are forced to respond, for we cannot view her with detachment. The artist's power awakens self-awareness and elicits sad agreement. As a Christian I grasp the truth about man's fallenness, my own included, with greater realism than from objective statements alone.

We could speak similarly about the truth in Graham Greene, Flannery O'Connor, and even Hemingway and Sartre. We may not like what we see and sometimes we find the truth distorted. But truth is not always beautiful, and neither is life, for the artist like the rest of us hovers between the fall of man and the eschaton, and he reveals what it is like to live there.

We can think of the painter and sculptor in similar ways. A look at contemporary visual arts makes plain that something has happened in modern life to man's image of himself and to the delight he once found in the world of nature. A painter-friend of mine says that artists no longer paint lakes or trees or flowers—or even people. The cubists and expressionists and neo-realists may paint human forms, but the person is missing from the body and the joys of creation are lacking in nature. In these regards the artist tells the truth about how modern man sees life: dehumanized, and for some, empty of meaning and joy.

Of course, there is considerably more to art than this. As in the case of philosophy other variables affect what the artist has done historically. He too wrestles with problems of a technical sort in his field. His methods change historically as new materials come into use and new techniques develop. And successive scientific models are just as evident in the history of painting as in the history of thought. We must be careful not to read into the work of a Mondrian or Picasso a view of life which they may not have shared with their more pessimistic peers, when in reality their work may be guided more by technical problems or by a choice of method and subject or by delighting in sensory effects than by the supposed truth of a nihilistic philosophy.

Yet the fact remains that cognitive truth as well as personal fidelity is present in art. Because it is the truth about how men perceive things, it reveals both what a man is like within himself and what the world looks like in which we live.

Because there is truth in art, and because imagination and creativity and beauty are God's good gifts, it follows that art, like nature and man and other domains of God's creation, may bear witness to the truth of God. Art may become as much a vehicle of general revelation as science and philosophy, for all truth is God's truth wherever it is found.

Does the Christian then have a mandate here? Wherever God's gifts are given, wherever in all creation truth can be seen, there a mandate exists to explore and bear witness to the truth and to invest ourselves for God's glory. Artistic appreciation and enjoyment and creativity are included.

(c) The loss of truth and of the Judaeo-Christian world-view is every bit as obvious in society at large as it is in education and the arts. The Christian has a mandate to emphasize *truth in society*, and to implement in the world that unity of truth which makes men free to live meaningfully.

We suffer today from the fact that too many decisions are made on purely pragmatic bases. If it works it must be right, we assume. And on that basis we have made money, raped natural resources, upset the ecological balance, fought wars, justified them with fabrications, perverted political and judicial processes, marketed inadequately tested goods, and deprived human beings of their rights. But when we probe the causes of political corruption, of crime and war and ecological crises, we must reject the optimism that thinks a rule of laws will finally prevail through men of good will. Until men come to love the right and love the truth with all their being, their societies can hardly be redeemed either.

To believe in truth is to love truth with one's whole being and to do the truth as well. For this reason, the Christian church is indeed the salt of the earth and a light in this world. But if the salt is to spread its savor and if the light is to shine and not be hid, then Christians must make their presence felt. By their work and other social involvements, they can and must bear witness to truth.

Once again, however, we must pause to remind ourselves that truth is not exclusively in Scripture, and witness to the truth cannot be limited to telling of Christ and the gospel. Undeniably, these are of central importance. But all truth is God's truth, wherever it be found, and this has implications for society.

These implications must be felt in the world of business and industry. The businessman should obey the law, of course, but should he not go the second mile when it comes to truth in advertising, to making and keeping contracts, to personnel policies, to production standards, and to his tax returns? The New Left scorned our plastic society for inundating us with petty baubles and convincing us that we need the trivia industry concocts. Where is the Christian conscience in such matters?

The laws allow many things that are not true to what is just and good, for the purpose of law is not to enforce morality, let alone a Christian ethic. But the Christian is called to bear witness to the truth even when the law allows otherwise. Legalizing abortion does not make every legal abortion right, and we may soon have to say the same of euthanasia, genetic engineering, and other new medical procedures. Some British medical researchers recently halted their work on extra-uterine conception, and, when one considers its moral dimensions, their caution may well be justified. The Christian of all people has responsibility to shape public opinion, to educate the Christian community, to let the truth be heard.

But the Christian's concern for truth in society need not always take a negative and critical form. We must do more than take exception. We must take initiative with creative plans and proposals that can help reshape society, at least in part. This calls for statesmanlike Christian leadership in business and industry, in law and medicine, in education and the arts. It calls for highly competent and highly principled Christians in local and national politics, seeking and exercising office because they believe in truth.

The idea of a Christian society is not new, nor is it the exclusive property of a liberal social gospel. T.S. Eliot and others wrote of it as they looked for a new world after World War II. Nineteenth century statesmen worked for it. The Puritans who colonized New England sought to establish it there, but it was Charlemagne's dream long before. Its roots lie deep in the history of Israel and their theocracy. It will only find perfect fulfilment in the millennial kingdom of which Scripture speaks, when the peoples of this world come to see that all truth is God's truth, and to obey the truth they see. Yet the ideal is not there to frustrate and disillusion us with the present world, but to motivate us to emphasize truth as fully as we possibly can in the world today. Perhaps the lion and the lamb cannot yet lie down together, but we can at least restrain the lion's violence while caring with compassion for the needs of both. Perhaps we cannot yet turn our spears into plowshares, but we can at least work for justice and compassion in our cities, for international understanding and cooperation, for arms limitation, for better priorities in national budgets.

But to act intelligently as Christians we must undergo a reformation of thought. Our concepts of love and marriage may need to be weaned further away from modern romantic notions, if truly Christian marriage is to be enjoyed. Our ideas of justice and of government will need the scrutiny of the Old Testament prophets if we are not to perpetuate the pitfalls of modern ideologies. Our attitudes to war and to rebellion, to criminal punishment and to economic development may all need revision. We can no longer assume, once we recognize the unity of truth in relation to God, that the traditional Western concepts our fathers held will do.

Such re-formation of thought demands that we think under the judgment of God's word, which is our only final rule of faith and conduct. It requires a process of learning that lasts far beyond the end of school or university. It will take humility, discipline, and dedication.

# Index of Subjects

**141**

# Index of Authors

# Index of Biblical References